American Men of Letters

BAYARD TAYLOR

Bayard Taylor

American Men of Letters

BAYARD TAYLOR

BY

ALBERT H. SMYTH

BOSTON AND NEW YORK

HOUGHTON MIFFLIN COMPANY

The Riverside Press Cambridge

PREFACE.

THE life of Bayard Taylor was so varied and so busy that a mere catalogue of his industry would fill a small volume. The most difficult part of my task has been to limit the narrative. I have therefore not attempted to follow him carefully in his travels, but have preferred to enter with more particularity into his literary history at home.

His biographer must continue to draw his materials from the " Life and Letters of Bayard Taylor," edited by Marie Hansen-Taylor and Horace E. Scudder. In addition to that admirable work I have had the advantage of examining the miscellaneous manuscript collections which Mrs. Taylor generously placed at my disposal. At every turn Bayard Taylor's friends and former colleagues have been kind and helpful. My thanks are due to Mr. Richard Henry Stoddard, Mr. Edmund Clarence Stedman, Rev. W. R. Alger, Mr. Parke Godwin, Mr. John Bigelow, Mr. Whitelaw Reid, Mr. Richard

213

Storrs Willis, Mr. H. S. Everett, Mr. Clinton Scollard, Hon. Andrew D. White, Hon. Samuel W. Pennypacker, and Professors James Morgan Hart and Waterman T. Hewett of Cornell University.

Mr. William D. Howells very kindly placed at my disposal the letters addressed by Bayard Taylor to him when he was editor of the " Atlantic Monthly."

The reminiscences of Mrs. Sara J. Lippincott (Grace Greenwood), Miss G. Bloede (Stuart Sterne), Mrs. Sidney Lanier, and Mrs. Annie Carey, a sister of Bayard Taylor, have been very useful to me.

I have particularly to thank my friends Mr. Donald G. Mitchell, Mr. William Winter, Mr. J. G. Rosengarten, Dr. Horace Howard Furness, and Mr. Thomas Bailey Aldrich, to whom I owe on this as on all other occasions gratitude heaped up and running over.

My page would be too small to contain the names of all the Chester County friends, who, out of their love and respect for Bayard Taylor, and the goodness of their generous hearts, showed me countless courtesies.

I must not fail, however, to mention Mr. James Monaghan of West Chester, and I cannot forget the constant interest and aid of my old preceptor and friend, Professor Daniel W. Howard.

As this is the first biography of a Pennsylvanian writer that has appeared in the Men of Letters Series, I have ventured to introduce a brief outline of literary history in Pennsylvania.

ALBERT H. SMYTH.

PHILADELPHIA, *November* 1, 1895.

CONTENTS.

BAYARD TAYLOR.

INTRODUCTION.

PENNSYLVANIA IN LITERATURE.

PENNSYLVANIA has not been well treated by the
historians of American literature. Only twelve
of the one hundred and sixty poets recorded in
" Griswold's Cemetery," as Dr. Holmes called
" The Poets and Poetry of America," are Penn-
sylvanians ; and in Duyckinck's " Cyclopædia "
the proportion is about the same. One facetious
critic defined Pennsylvania as " a State more
famous for its coal and iron than for its literature," and another declared that her most famous
men were Benjamin Franklin and Albert Gal-
latin : the one a native of Massachusetts, the
other of Geneva.

Yet, turning these jests out of service, the
time was when Philadelphia, the Federal City,
was the centre of the nation's literary life.
Pennsylvania had then so far allured Coleridge
and Southey as to give a local habitation to

their dreams of a Pantisocracy upon the Susquehanna ; Wyoming, although mispronounced by
Campbell, had a permanent place in English
literature ; and at least two English poets —
Scott and Campbell — had proved michers and
appropriated tempting lines from Philadelphia
poets.

As the old capital of American literature,
Philadelphia was commonly called " the American Athens " long before the title was coveted
by Boston. The best library in the country
in colonial times was owned in Philadelphia by
James Logan, who had books " so scarce that
neither price nor prayers could purchase them."
Through the practical thoughtfulness of such
men as Franklin, and Hopkinson, and Robert
Grace, the city possessed the first circulating
library in the colonies. One hundred years ago
the American Academy in Boston was the only
scientific foundation within the Republic that
was not in Philadelphia. In politics and poetry
Pennsylvania led the country. " The Farmer's
Letters " of John Dickinson were the ablest and
most efficient political forces of the pre-revolutionary period, and they determined the principles
of the Revolution. William Cliffton, a native of
Southwark, in Philadelphia, wrote the best verse
produced in America in the eighteenth century.
The earliest American drama, " The Prince of

Parthia," was the work of Thomas Godfrey, a Philadelphian and son of the inventor of the quadrant.

The profession of letters began in this country with Charles Brockden Brown, whose ancestors had come to Philadelphia with William Penn in the Welcome. It is a singular chapter of literary history that finds in Shelley's interest in Brown's romances the impulse to the authorship of "Zastrozzi" and "St. Irvyne." Contemporary with Brown, and his successor in the literary guild, Joseph Dennie, "the American Addison," found his congenial home in Philadelphia, and drew about him in the Tuesday Club, and as contributors to the "Port-Folio," nearly two-score cultivated Philadelphia gentlemen, some of whom have since been writ large in our literary annals, while others have disappeared into the oblivion they merited. The press in Philadelphia was active and bold. It gave to the country, in nearly every case, the first American editions of the classics, and of notable English writers. Joseph Hopkinson edited the first, and Joseph Dennie annotated the second American edition of Shakespeare ; Robert Bell printed the first Milton, and Robert Aitken the first English Bible. The long catalogue of minor publications practically registers the culture of the nation.

Nearly every experiment in periodical litera-

ture was first tried in Philadelphia, from the
first monthly magazine to the first daily newspaper. Even after the removal of the seat of
government, and the vanishing of the cosmopolitan character that for a time had given to the
city the air of foreign capitals, Philadelphia's
literary preëminence continued to draw to it the
writers of New York and of New England.
Hawthorne makes Holgrave in " The House of
the Seven Gables " say, " My name has figured,
I can assure you, on the covers of Graham and
Godey, making as respectable an appearance,
for aught I could see, as any of the canonized
bead-roll with which it was associated." Nearly
every memorable name in our literature confesses
some connection with the Philadelphia press.
Edgar Allan Poe and James Russell Lowell
were editorial writers upon " Graham's Magazine," John Greenleaf Whittier edited " The
Pennsylvania Freeman," and Washington Irving
conducted " The Analectic Magazine."

Pennsylvania furnishes some curious phenomena of social history. Nowhere is there a more
varied commingling of nationalities : English,
Scotch, Irish, Welsh, Dutch, Swedes, Nor-
wegians, Danes,[1] French, and Germans. In the
" Urlsperger Nachrichten " (Halle, 1735) there
is a summary of this amazing variety of blood

[1] Planted by Ole Bull in 1853.

and creed : " Diese Stadt ist sehr florisant. . . .
Es ist hier ein Sitz von allen Religionen und
Secten, Lutheranern, Reformirten, Bischöfli-
chen, Presbyterianern, Catholicken, Quackern,
Dümplern, Mennonisten, Sabbatheriens, Sieben-
tagern, Separatisten, Böhmisten, Schwenkfeld-
ianern, Tuchtfelder, Wohlwünscher, Juden, und
Heyden."

The counties lying west of the Susquehanna
River along the Maryland line are inhabited by
Germans speaking a *patois* made up of the
speech of the Rhenish palatinate and an admixture of English words and phrases. It is a
dialect without a literature. The only literary
examples it possesses are humorous experiments
made by philological students. The translation
of " Hamlet " into Pennsylvania Dutch has been
made memorable by its rendering of " I am
thy father's ghost " into the grotesque " Ich bin
deim dawdy, sei spook." Henry Harbaugh in
" S'alt Schulhaus an der Krick " has humorously portrayed the provincial life. Of genuine
German literature there is very little in the
State, but a poem by a Moravian minister in
Bethlehem had the honor of fixing Goethe's
thought for a time upon Pennsylvania and of
eliciting from him some remarkable verse. Pastor Gregor addressed to his daughter on her
eleventh birthday a poetic epistle, " Aus Bethle-

hem nach Herrenhut." Its quaint language
and naïve sentiment held the attention of Goethe,
who wrote a parallel to it, "Nicht am Susquehanna ;" both the original epistle and the parallel are printed in volume forty-seven of the
1833 edition of Goethe.[1]

The Scotch-Irish who were originally centred
about Lancaster, Paxton, and Hanover have
now gone farther westward. With all their
personal force, and good qualities as pioneers,
they were bare of sentiment and barren of imagination ; and in Pennsylvania, as elsewhere,
showed themselves unable to shake off their
sterile curse. Two only of this strain contributed to Pennsylvanian literature : H. H. Bracken-
ridge of Carlisle, who wrote "Modern Chivalry,"
the first satirical novel, and D. Bruce of Washington County, the lonely poet of his race.[2]

Southern Lancaster, Southern Chester, and
Delaware counties have been for two hundred
years occupied by English Quakers, the most
intelligent population in the State, and the
descendants for the most part of Penn's colonists.
The territory which they have occupied is the

[1] The Susquehanna flows freely through European literature, but nowhere more sweetly than in Nicolaus Lenau's *Der
Indianerzug.* In American poetry Dr. Caleb Harlan's *El-
flora of the Susquehanna* will be remembered.

[2] *Poems chiefly in the Scottish Dialect, originally written
under the signature of the Scots-Irishman,* Washington, 1801.

great limestone plain extending to within twenty miles of Philadelphia. It is a land of old and rare beauty, of rich farms and old families. It is a rolling country, perpetually diversified ; its pastoral loveliness, its wooded slopes, and narrow valleys continually recall the scenery of midland England. The roads go curling and curving along the flanks of low hills, and by the wayside creep the trim hedges of osage-orange.

Men and women from woody Warwickshire built the comfortable stone houses upon the fat farms in this mellow land, and here they lived their simple lives, morally austere, —

"Seeing the sternness of life, but, alas ! overlooking its graces."

Simplicity of manners, loyalty to truth, justice, peace, and humanity are the virtues reverenced and practiced by the Quakers. But their lives were not adorned and enlarged by the refining influences of the gentle arts. Their sense of art was dull. They hung no pictures upon their blank walls, nor listened to the touches of sweet harmony. No line of beauty ever disturbed the grave and stern decorum of their sober meeting-houses. It is not an advantage to any lover of the arts to have two or three generations of Quaker ancestry. Bernard Barton, the Quaker poet of England, before he published a volume of verse, consulted with

Robert Southey as to the propriety of his project, for he feared mightily the censure of his
friends for devoting himself to poetry. Whittier, when making his " Songs of Three Centuries," found it necessary to omit, though with
some heaviness of heart, the best and most characteristic examples of Thomas Campbell, because
they were battle-pieces. There were books and
learning among the Friends ; but the unbending
moral austerity, the narrow grooves in which
their lives ran, the *repression* that stamped their
faces and their characters, the little oddities
and prejudices for which they passionately con-
tended, were an unpromising soil for literature
to flourish in.

About 1820 the prestige of Philadelphia as a
literary centre began to fade. In the periodicals
of that period is to be detected an accent of
discontent and fear, rising sometimes into a note
of alarm. As new lights shine out in New England and in New York the jealous editor of the
" Port-Folio " writes, " With such rivalry Philadelphia must yield the proud title which she has
borne, or rouse from the withering lethargy in
which she slumbers." The conservatism that
was fostered by the Quaker temper, and by the
spirit that was alien to art, was in no small
measure responsible for the decline of literary
activity. New York was responsive to the new

forces and influences in literature. Philadelphia clung to the traditions that bore sway when the colony was young. Wordsworth made Bryant, and Cooper followed Scott; Philadelphia laughed at all the Goths of the romantic school, and continued to draw her poetry from Pope and her prose from Addison. " William Wordsworth," said the " Port-Folio " in 1809, " stands among the foremost of those English bards who have mistaken silliness for simplicity, and with a false and affected taste filled their papers with the language of children and clowns." [1]

The resistance to new ideas which William Cliffton at the time of Jay's treaty had lamented as one of the characteristics of Pennsylvania, and which had become more pronounced after the disappearance of the foreign society from Philadelphia, would have been enough in itself to chill the literary spirit and to bring to nothing its endeavor, but the passing of the sceptre was greatly accelerated by the opening in 1825 of the Erie Canal and the settlement of the West by way of New York.

It is interesting to note that at this time, when

---

[1] At a later period, indeed, Henry Reed was the ablest interpreter of Wordsworth, and George Allen the most learned disciple of Coleridge, but the former was too soon lost in the wreck of the Arctic, and the genius of the latter was rather critical than creative, and his influence chiefly pedagogic and theological.

the feuilletonists were in despair for Pennsylvania, four of the chief poets of the State, in four successive years, were born: T. Buchanan Read, in Chester County, in 1822, George Henry Boker, in Philadelphia, in 1823, Charles Godfrey Leland, in Philadelphia, in 1824, and Bayard Taylor, in Chester County, in 1825.

Bayard Taylor's faith and discipline were rooted in Quaker reason and practice. But he was German as well as English, and the Teutonic strain saved him from the icy current and compulsive course to which his surroundings seemed to consign him.

" Was it my fault, if a strain of the distant and dead generations
Rose in my being, renewed, and made me other than these are?
Purer, perhaps, their habit of law than the freedom they
      shrink from ;
So, restricted by will, a little indulgence is riot.
They, content with the glow of a carefully tempered twilight,
Measured pulses of joy, and colorless growth of the senses,
Stand aghast at my dream of the sun, and the sound, and the
      splendor!
Mine it is, and remains, resenting the threat of suppression,
Stubbornly shaping my life, and feeding with fragments its
      hunger,
Drifted from Attican hills to stray on a Scythian level, —
So unto me it appears, — unto them a perversion and scandal."

Bayard Taylor's life is so closely interwoven with the social conditions of Pennsylvania that the foregoing brief recital of his racial and cultural surroundings seems indispensable to a proper appreciation or interpretation. That he was allied by kindred blood to Pastor Gregor's people is the explanation of the Goethe studies, the translation of " Faust," and the ministry to Germany. Without the inherited conservatism, energy, and thrift of the Cheshire Taylors and Wiltshire Mendenhalls he never would have built Cedarcroft, nor taken the wind of the world in all its moods.

CHAPTER I.

BAYARD TAYLOR was just as old as the railway. He was born at Kennett Square, Chester County, Pennsylvania, in a two-story stone house, not now standing, on the eleventh of January, 1825, " the year when the first locomotive successfully performed its trial trip."

His father, Joseph Taylor, was a direct descendant in the sixth generation of Robert Taylor of Little Leigh, Cheshire, who came over with William Penn, and settled near the Brandywine Creek. The family lived obedient to Quaker principles until Bayard's grandfather, John Taylor, married Ann Bucher, daughter of Christian Bucher, a Swiss Mennonite of Lancaster County, and granddaughter of Melchior Breneman, a Mennonite minister whose grandfather came from Switzerland in the Mennonite emigration of 1709, and took up a large tract of land south of the present city of Lancaster. For refusing to say that he was sorry for his runaway love match, John Taylor was expelled from meeting.

A second strain of German blood Bayard Taylor inherited from his grandmother on the mother's side, who was of South German or East Switzerland origin. To this infusion of a foreign element Taylor refers in "The Palm and the Pine:" —

> "For, as a fountain disappears,
>   To gush again in later years,
>
> "So hidden blood may find the day,
>   When centuries have rolled away;
>
> "And fresher lives betray at last
>   The lineage of a far-off Past.
>
> "That nature, mixed of sun and snow,
>   Repeats its ancient ebb and flow:
>
> "The children of the Palm and Pine
>   Renew their blended lives — in mine."

Doubtless to his German stock was due the strong attraction that Teutonic studies had for him, and to it he was wont to trace his "Lust zu fabuliren."

Joseph Taylor and Rebecca Way were married in Brandywine Township, October 15, 1818. Bayard Taylor was the fourth child of this marriage, and the first to outlive infancy. Through his mother, who was a granddaughter

of Rebecca (Mendenhall) Way, he was related
to the ancient family of the Mendenhalls whose
ancestral home was the manor of Mildenhall
in Wiltshire.   Benjamin Mendenhall came to
Pennsylvania with William Penn, and settled at
Concord, in what is now Delaware County. His
daughter Anne became the second wife of John
Bartram, whom Linnæus cited as the greatest
natural botanist in the world.

Although Joseph Taylor was not a member
of the Society of Friends, his children were instructed in Quaker manners and beliefs, and
upon Quaker principles the steadfast faith and
simple morals of Bayard Taylor rested. His
mother's earnest teaching of non-resistance and
the sin of swearing had its legitimate fruit in
" the chastity of temperate blood " and " the settled faith that nothing shakes." Once, after a
homily upon swearing, the lad was seized with
such a desire to swear that he went forth alone
into a field, and there " snatched a fearful joy "
by cleansing his stuffed bosom of all the perilous oaths he had ever heard. The childish
mutiny was a portent of his future rebellion
against the " pious Quaker repression " of which
he speaks in " Home Pastorals."

"Weary am I with all this preaching the force of example,
Painful duty to self, and painfuller still to one's neighbor,
Moral shibboleths, dinned in one's ears with slavering unction,
Till, for the sake of a change, profanity loses its terrors."

Out of admiration for Senator James A. Bayard of Delaware, Joseph and Rebecca Taylor gave his chivalric and poetic name to their son, who in his youth wrote his name J. Bayard Taylor, but a few years after coming of age wisely discarded the first initial. The family moved in 1829 to a farm which was a part of the original land-grant made to Robert Taylor by William Penn ; it was in East Marlborough Township, one mile from Kennett Square. Humble means and fresh country air are perhaps the most fortunate endowments of young genius, and to the free and active life of Hazeldell Farm Bayard Taylor was indebted for the robust health that enabled him to carry forward his great burden of tasks, and for the buoyant spirits that made him, like a holy witch, enchant societies unto him.

If his childhood was remarkable for anything, it was for a roving disposition that led him to strange explorations, and for a fondness for making collections from nature. " Almost my first recollection," he wrote in " At Home and Abroad," " is of a swamp, into which I went bare-legged at morning, and out of which I came, when driven by hunger, with long stockings of black mud, and a mask of the same. . . . The treasures I there collected were black terrapins with orange spots, baby frogs the size of a chestnut, thrushes' eggs, and stems of purple phlox." As a lad of fourteen he rose to the higher dignity of making a mineralogical collection and a herbarium.

He learned to read when he was four years old, and the passion for books that began with "Captain Riley's Narrative," and "Peter Parley," and Scott's poetry, and Gibbon's "Rome," and was whetted by the two hundred volumes of the Kennett library, passed almost instantly and imperceptibly into the enthusiasm for authorship. He was seven years of age when he wrote his first poems, and added them to the neat copies that he had made of Scott and Campbell. When the news of Byron's death reached England, Tennyson, then a lad of fifteen, crept away into a lonely glen of Lincolnshire, and in the bitterness of grief carved upon a rock, "Byron is dead!" A like passion for literature and for men of letters possessed the boy Taylor, and among his earliest memories the deaths, in 1832, of Goethe and Scott held high and sacred place. His fondness for books and reading and his dislike of the farm labor brought him at times beneath his father's frown. Hawthorne at Brook Farm, with a shiver of disgust, said that he had expected to live in Arcady and found himself up to the chin in a barnyard; in like manner Taylor's delicately adjusted nervous or-

ganization shrank from the coarse and homely
duties of the garden and the field, and his mother had frequently to screen him by employing
him to ply some light task within the house.
He worked industriously at many things, sometimes drying and selling lobelia and sumac, in
order to obtain pocket money whereby to in-
crease his little store of books.

One of the distressful strokes his youth suffered was on the day that it became his duty to
ride to the mill and to bring home the heavy
flour bags which would persist in falling off,
whereupon he would sit in mute despair beside
the giant sacks and await the coming of a
stronger arm. He was, withal, full of fun and
mischief. The tricks and pranks of Joe and
Jake Fairthorn in "The Story of Kennett" are
Taylor's recollections of his own boyhood, as
when he frightened the old Swiss servant, Vic-
torine, into shrieking "Christus, Marie, und
Joseph!" by his horrified report of his brother's
imaginary fall from the big cherry-tree ("Story
of Kennett," p. 51).

He was sent in his sixth year to a dame's
school kept by Ruth Anne Chambers. It was
a little log schoolhouse with a chestnut grove
behind it. "His way thither was through a
lonely meadow on his father's farm, and a piece
of woodland." He retained an abiding recol-

lection of the terrors he felt in running in the
darkness of the wood and fearfully listening to
the rush of the wind. Wordsworth's "Wanderer" at like age had

> "Traveled through the woods with no one near
> To whom he might confess the things he saw."

And so the foundations of Taylor's mind were
laid : —

> "In such communion not from terror free,
> While yet a child, and long before his time
> Had he perceived the presence and the power
> Of greatness."

Another school to which he was put was on
the Toughkenamon road, — a locality afterwards
celebrated in "The Story of Kennett," — and
was kept by Samuel Martin. The love of color
which later was to light up his pictures of tropical scenery then found its juvenile expression in
drawing and painting. He illustrated his verse-
book in colors, and made drawings of "Byron's
Dream" and other poetic rhapsodies. When
he came to write "The Picture of St. John,"
and dedicated the work to the artists he had
known, he expressed, in rather juvenile verse, a
half regret for this untraveled roadway in his
life.

> "And though some sportive nymph the channel turned
> And led to other fields mine infant rill,
> The sense of fancied destination still
> Leaps in its waves, and will not be unlearned.

> I charge not Fate with having done me wrong ;
> Much hath she granted, though so much was spurned;
> But leave the keys of Color silent long,
> And pour my being through the stops of song."

So genuine was this instinct for art, that in 1839 he addressed a letter to the distinguished engraver, Mr. John Sartain, asking to be received as an apprentice; and the impulse to painting, in 1840, was as strong with him as it had been with Allston and with Read.

Joseph Taylor was elected sheriff of Chester County in 1837, and the family for the three years following resided at West Chester, where Bayard went to Bolmar's Academy. Dr. Thomas Dunn English of Philadelphia, at that time unknown as an author, and newly graduated from the medical school of the University of Pennsylvania, lectured in West Chester in the summer of 1839 upon phrenology. The Quaker with his "inward light" and openness to all spiritual influences listened attentively to the presentation of the theories of Mesmer, and of Gall, and Spurzheim. The morning after the lecture Dr. English, at the invitation of his friend and fellow-alumnus, Dr. Hartman, who later acquired fame as a conchologist, visited the jail and greatly amused Sheriff Taylor by examining the formation of heads and casting characters and dispositions. "After it was through " (writes Dr. English to me in a letter of December 14, 1894), " we passed into the office. There was a lank, long-legged, half-grown boy seated on a high stool, and the sheriff said, ' There is my son; what do you think of him? I propose to make a farmer out of him. Do you think he is fitted for it?' I took a glance at the head, which was a very marked one, and said, ' You will never make a farmer of him to any great extent: you will never keep him home; that boy will ramble around the world, and furthermore, he has all the marks of a poet.' At this the sheriff laughed immensely. The sheriff's name was Taylor, and this was his son Bayard, afterwards traveler, poet, and minister to Berlin." This story was first told in the West Chester local paper by Dr. W. D. Hartman, who is the original of the old physician in " Joseph and his Friend." Bayard was at this time fourteen years old, and Dr. English had curiously divined the two controlling instincts of his life. Already his reading had taken two directions, and poetry and travels were eagerly sought after. From his seventh year he composed poetry, mostly by way of imitation, and in 1841 a " Soliloquy of a Young Poet," his first published poem, appeared in the " Saturday Evening Post." When he was seventeen he was enthusiastic over Bryant, and

Longfellow, and Whittier, and Lowell, — "all
Americans, you know," he wrote to J. B. Phillips, — and he felt the greatest sorrow at the
death of Channing (1842), "as much so, perhaps, as if he were a near and dear friend." His
earliest prose themes were travels, or at least
descriptions of foreign and romantic scenes.
His schoolfellows ridiculed him for his dreams
of travel. George Macdonald represents one
of his heroes, a wanderer in the world, as possessed with the instinctive desire to climb to the
summits of the highest hills and to the top of
tallest steeples to look abroad over wide stretches
of country. The same passion was in Taylor
from childhood. He wrote in "At Home and
Abroad:" "In looking back to my childhood I
can recall the intensest desire to climb upward,
so that without shifting the circle of my horizon,
I could yet extend it, and take in a far wider
sweep of vision. I envied every bird that sat
swinging upon the topmost bough of the great
century-old cherry-tree; the weathercock on our
barn seemed to me to whirl in a higher region
of the air; and to rise from the earth in a bal-
loon was a bliss which I would almost have
given my life to enjoy."

Shortly before the sheriff's term of service
expired and the family returned to Kennett,
Bayard Taylor was sent (1839–40) to Unionville

Academy, where he received the last of his schooling. Unionville is an interesting village of three hundred inhabitants, built upon high banks along the State Road, a highway that continues the Lancaster Pike from Philadelphia to Oxford. The little houses with porches and round pillars are completely embowered in trees. At the east end of the town stands the ivy-covered house of Martha Deane celebrated in "The Story of Kennett." At the opposite end is the schoolhouse, now enlarged and translated into a high school, where fifty years ago Jonathan Gause bore his mild sway; and in its new belfry swings the old bell that rang when Taylor was a student, and whose clear tones can be heard on favorable days in Kennett, four miles away. In 1840 Unionville was a bustling place. It was an important cattle-market; often a thousand head of cattle were sold in a day. Bayard Taylor while a student must have seen the great cattle from the Western Reserve and the small kine from Maryland driven into the town; and among the drovers from a West Virginian farm he may have seen a tall spare youth, one year his senior, who was destined to win high fame in American history and to bear the name of "Stonewall" Jackson.

Jonathan Gause was thorough in his methods, and successful in his teaching. From his

Academy Dr. Isaac Hayes, the arctic explorer, was graduated, and among Taylor's fellow students were John Smith Futhey and R. E. Monaghan, both of whom became prominent in good works in Chester County.

These three friends made a tramp trip, April 5, 1840, from Unionville to the battlefield of the Brandywine. It was the first of Taylor's travels, and the account of it which appeared in the same year in the "West Chester Register" was his first publication. At this time he was studying Latin and French and conning such native Chester County text-books as Lewis's Algebra and Gummere's Surveying. German he had already in part acquired from Wieland's "Oberon," and from his grandmother and the Swiss servant of the family.

His verbal memory and his facility in rhymes were chiefly noticeable. Gause applauded his quickness, and set him upon memorizing poems and orations, which he accomplished in an astonishingly short time. His memory was not only quick but tenacious, and the poems committed in childhood remained with him through life. Indeed, as was the case with Macaulay, the retentiveness of his memory was not always a blessing, for it was as indiscriminate in its appropriations as it was unyielding in its grasp. He was forever composing acrostics on his fellow

students and caricaturing them in rhymes and
in drawings, and this pert and nimble spirit of
mirth continued with him through life, prompt-
ing him to innocent mischief and making him
the sunniest companion in every social group.
He was well aware that he had no prospect of
collegiate education, and he made the most of
his time at Unionville. His restless intellect
was supported by abundant physical health.
He enjoyed the raptures of intellectual excitement. He was thrilled with the aspirations
which his reading kindled ; and the great world
of literature stood before him, — the paradise
of his constant endeavor. He addressed a letter to Charles Dickens which brought an autograph reply, and in consequence the lad was
caught up into the seventh heaven of ecstasy.
" I can long recollect the thrill of pleasure I experienced on seeing the autograph of one whose
writings I so ardently admired and to whom, in
spirit, I felt myself attached ; and it was not
without a feeling of ambition that I looked upon
it that as he, an humble clerk, had risen to be
the guest of a mighty nation, so I, an humble
pedagogue, might, by unremitted and arduous
intellectual and moral exertion, become a light,
a star, among the names of my country. May
it be ! "

No doubt when he came to write " John God-

frey's Fortunes," which is more than " a story
of American life," as he calls it, for it is really
a fragment of his autobiography, he reverted in
affectionate memory to those early thrills and
aspirations when the world of letters was the
ideal world, and authors occupied sacred places
in his rapt Pantheon. It is of the publication of
his first poem in the " Saturday Evening Post "
of Philadelphia, when he was sixteen years of
age, that he is thinking when he makes John
Godfrey say : " My intention had been to deliver the letter at the office of the paper as if I
had been simply its bearer and not its author.
But after I had mounted two dark steep flights
of steps, and found myself before the door,
my courage failed me. I heard voices within :
there were several persons, then. They would
be certain to look at me sharply — to notice my
agitation — perhaps to question me about the
letter. While I was standing thus, twisting and
turning it in my hand, in a veritable perspi-
ration from excitement, I heard footsteps descending from an upper story. Desperate and
panic-stricken, I laid the letter hastily on the
floor, at the door of the office, and rushed down
to the street as rapidly and silently as possible.
Without looking around, I walked up Chestnut
Street with a fearful impression that somebody
was following me, and, turning the corner of

Fourth, began to read the titles of the books in Hart's window. Five minutes having elapsed, I knew that I was not discovered, and recovered my composure, though, now that the poem had gone out of my hands, I would have given anything to get it back again.

" When the next number of the paper arrived, I tore off the wrapper with trembling fingers and turned to the fateful column on the second page. But I might as well have postponed my excitement: there was no notice of the poem. Perhaps they had never received the letter — perhaps it had been trodden upon and defaced, and swept down stairs by the office boy ! These were, at least, consoling possibilities, — better that than to be contemptuously ignored. By the following week my fever was nearly over, and I opened the paper with but a faint expectation of finding anything ; but lo ! there it was — ' Selim ' at the very head of the announcements ! These were the precious words : ' We are obliged to " Selim " for his poem, which we shall publish shortly. It shows the hand of youth, but evinces a flattering promise. Let him trim the midnight lamp with diligence.'

" If the sinking sun had wheeled about and gone up the western sky, or the budding trees had snapped into full leaf in five minutes, I don't believe it would have astonished me. I was on

my way home from the post-office when I read
the lines, and I remember turning out of Penn
Street to go by a more secluded and circuitous
way, lest I should be tempted to cut a pigeon-
wing on the pavement in the sight of the multitude. I passed a little brick building, with a tin
sign on the shutter, — 'D. J. Mulford, Attorney
at Law.' 'Pooh!' I said to myself; 'what's
D. J. Mulford? He never published a poem in
his life!' As I caught a glimpse of his head,
silhouetted against the back window, I found
myself, nevertheless, rather inclined to pity him
for being unconscious that the author of 'The
Unknown Bard' was at that moment passing
his door." [1]

While he thus lived in fantasy, and dreamed
great dreams, his connection with Unionville, as
student and as tutor, ceased (March 26, 1842),
and he went back to the farm. Upon his right
hand, as he journeyed away from the place where
the eager currents of his young life had been
restrained, lay the farm to which he was later
to give literary interest by his ballad of "John
Reed." And perhaps, enthusiastic as he was,
had he stopped to ponder upon the coming years
he would have anticipated the sad strain of the
ballad : —

[1] Bayard Taylor's poem *The Nameless Bard* was published
in *Graham's Magazine*, August, 1843.

"It's the hankering after a life that you never have learned to
     know,
It's the discontent with a life that is always thus and so ;
It's the wondering what we are, and where we are going to go."

He remained at home but a few weeks. He
was no better satisfied than he had been in childhood with the labor of the farm, and his father
consented to apprentice him for four years to
Henry S. Evans, printer, in West Chester. In
May he began his new life as a compositor in the
" Village Record" office, and boarded with the
other apprentices in Henry Evans's house upon
the Strasburgh road. There was culture in
West Chester and there were libraries. The
intellectual curiosity of the people was rather
toward science than literature. The study of
plants and shells and minerals was placed higher
than the gift of graceful expression. The lad
who was helped with his herbarium and his min-
eral cabinet was discouraged from poetry and
romance. The severe practicality of the Penn-
sylvanians, both English and German, led to the
achievements of Humphrey Marshall and Gott-
hilf Muhlenberg, the Bartrams and the Dar-
lingtons, and in our own day has awarded the
highest scientific honors to the Pennsylvania
German Dr. Leidy, and the English Pennsylva-
nians Cope and Brinton.

" The Village Record" was a good school.

It had a literary tradition. Its former editor, Charles Miner, who wrote the history of Wyoming, had been gifted with some sense of literary form and perspective, and he had given character and quality to the articles in his paper. Many of Taylor's fellows in apprenticeship have filled places of use and of renown. They are editors and jurists, and one has been chief justice of the State.

As a lad of seventeen Taylor was six feet in height, straight, athletic, full of life, with dark brown eyes and hair. He was full of magnetism to his finger tips. Mesmerism reached West Chester in his adolescence and he was singularly successful in his experiments with it. This personal fascination never entirely left him. A subtle influence went forth from him that attracted men to him, and stole their hearts away. Upon the Nile the boatmen followed him with their eyes, and were prompt to render him, without thought of reward, any service in their way. He tells in " Views Afoot " the pretty story of a child who broke from its playmates and their game to run across the street and catch his hand and look up with a trusting smile into his handsome face.

While in West Chester he read Herder, in German, with Miss Evans ; and resumed his studies in Spanish with Mrs. Evans and with

Canizares, a Spaniard. With William Butler, now a judge of the United States District Court and Morris Ingram, a former school-fellow at Unionville, he organized a society called "The Thespians," and they gave recitations and dramatic performances in the Odd Fellows Hall over the "Record" office.

Some verses that he had contributed to the "Saturday Evening Post," particularly the lines "To the Brandywine," brought him to the notice of Rufus W. Griswold, then editor of "Graham's Magazine" and who had just published his "Poets and Poetry of America." Griswold was a power in those days, and his favor was anxiously solicited by young writers, and his countenance coveted by older ones. His circle of acquaintance included all the *literati* of the country, and his arrogant air made his little literature seem stately and imposing. "Ruffian Griswold" those called him who had felt the weight of his disapproval, but to many who in evident sincerity solicited his aid he extended a helping hand. "Graham's Magazine" was made by George R. Graham in 1841 by a combination of Atkinson's "Casket" and Burton's "Gentleman's Magazine." Its "canonized beadroll" contained the names of nearly all the well-known writers of the country. Cooper and Poe, Longfellow and Hawthorne were con-

stant contributors; and the names of " Fanny
Forester," Alice and Phœbe Cary, " Grace
Greenwood," Frances S. Osgood, N. P. Willis,
James K. Paulding, Park Benjamin, Charles
Fenno Hoffman, Alfred B. Street, and Albert
Pike figured frequently upon its covers. Wash-
ington Irving alone, wholly occupied with the
" Knickerbocker Magazine," had no connection
with " Graham's."

Into this choice companionship of literary
names Taylor was admitted through the kindly
interest of Griswold, and, encouraged by the
Philadelphia autocrat, he began to cherish
" hopes of occupying at some future day a
respectable station among our country's poets."
Griswold strongly advised him to publish a
poetic romance that he had been engaged upon
for a considerable time, together with other of
his poems, in a volume. Mistrusting his own
inclination and judgment, Taylor, with his customary candor, submitted his verses to a few
trusted friends; and as no serious attempt was
made to dissuade him from an enterprise which,
however, did not promise any particular gain or
benefit, he began to solicit subscriptions, and
early in February, 1844, appeared " Ximena;
| or | The Battle of the Sierra Morena, | and |
other Poems, | By James Bayard Taylor. | ' I
am a Youthful Traveler in the Way.' Henry

Kirk White | Philadelphia : | Herman Hooker, 178 Chesnut Street | MDCCCXLIV. |

It was dedicated to Rufus W. Griswold, "As an expression of gratitude for the kind encouragement he has shown the author." Bryant had published " The Embargo " when fourteen years of age, and a few other American poets had lisped in numbers more or less musical, but the firmament was not then crowded with literary lights, and it was a thing more unusual than now for a lad of nineteen to send forth a volume of verse. It brought him some pleasant letters and a little money, and gave him in popular repute a place among the poets.

Never did youth entertain fairer visions of fame than were the possession at this time of this West Chester lad ; never did man have higher and more abstracted ambition ; never did a generous and gentle nature pant more eagerly for recognition and for sympathy. Upon the fly-leaf of a copy of " Ximena " presented to Lowell, as of one presented to Longfellow, are the words, " From his stranger-friend, J. Bayard Taylor." The letter that accompanied the presentation to Lowell read : "Will you receive the offering of a bard unknown to you, as a small return for the spiritual enjoyment you have given him ? I am but a youth, and have a life of toil before me, and whenever I weary of my

burden, the voice of the Poet, prophet-like, bids
me ' suffer and be strong.' I dare not as yet
call myself a Brother-Bard; but I send you the
first breathings of my soul, with the ardent
hope they will find a response in your own."

It was a boy's letter, and the book was a boy's
book. Too early publication is always a vain
regret. Taylor in after years repudiated the
fifteen poems that constituted the little volume,
and wished them forgotten. There are constant
recollections in them of the author's reading;
and to the faint lyrical faculty that he already
displayed is superadded a very evident affection
for the manner of Scott, and Byron, and Moore,
and Mrs. Hemans. It is interesting to note the
boy Taylor looking about him for the subjects
of his song. He does not sigh his breath in
foreign clouds, nor celebrate the skylark or the
bulbul. He knows his native grounds and
loves them, and he writes poems upon Pennsylvania and Catskill and indites verses " To the
Brandywine." [1]

[1] It has hitherto passed without notice that the earliest publication by T. Buchanan Read was a novel whose persons and
places are all to be found between Philadelphia and Lancaster.
It is *Paul Redding: A Tale of the Brandywine*, printed in
Boston in 1845. Read ripples into verse amid his narrative
when he praises —

> " The bright, the laughing Brandywine
> That dallies with its hundred mills."

"Ximena" was published not all so much for fame, as for another close intent which Taylor meant to reach unto. His reading had "clothed foreign countries with a splendid atmosphere of poetry and art." The longing for travel in those realms of gold began with his acquaintance at ten years with Willis's "Pencillings by the Way." The longing became a steadfast resolve with the reading of "Hyperion." The doubts created by those to whom he applied for information, and who named prohibitory sums as the inevitable expenses of the journey, were dissipated by Howitt's "Rural Life in Germany," which confirmed him in his belief that the journey might be made very cheaply on foot.

Still it seemed impossible to procure the money that was necessary. The project appeared to his friends and neighbors wild and visionary. He realized and resented the repression of all that was dearest to him so inevitable in the community which surrounded him. When he reflected upon the impossibility of satisfying his ambition at home, he said that he felt as if he were sitting in an exhausted receiver while the air which should nourish his spiritual life could only be found in distant lands. While he was negotiating for the publication of "Ximena" he frequently walked the

thirty miles from Kennett to Philadelphia, and
in these lonely walks he was occupied in fancy
with the strong conflict between his desire to
travel abroad into the world, and the affection
and sense of duty to which his friends and
family appealed to hold him still within the
narrow life of home. Concerning one of these
occasions he wrote to his friend Phillips : " I
sat down by the roadside, for it was then dark,
and looking to heaven through my blinding
tears, fervently prayed for strength of spirit to
sustain me in my conflict with the world. And
the struggle in my breast ceased, and I felt
that the path which was to lead me onward and
upward was that which was the desire of my
soul." His first step was to buy the remainder
of his apprenticeship time from Mr. Evans.
Two weeks before the day fixed upon for leaving home he had secured no employment and
did not possess a dollar toward his outfit. He
then walked to Philadelphia, and spent two or
three days calling upon the principal editors
and publishers of the city. " At last " (he
wrote in the introductory chapter to " Views
Afoot "), " when I was about to return home,
not in despair, but in a state of wonder as to
where my funds would come from (for I felt
certain they *would* come), Mr. Patterson, at
that time publisher of the ' Saturday Evening

Post,' offered me fifty dollars in advance for twelve letters, with the promise of continuing the engagement, if the letters should be satisfactory. The Hon. Joseph R. Chandler, editor of the ' United States Gazette,' then made me a similar offer." Mr. Graham paid with his wonted liberality for some manuscript poems, and the delighted boy returned in triumph to Kennett with a fund of one hundred and forty dollars. He was entirely ignorant of the proceedings necessary to procure a passport, and supposed he was obliged to report himself at the national capital. Accordingly he and his cousin, Franklin Taylor, set forth for Washington, a distance of one hundred miles. They walked to Port Deposit, on the Susquehanna River, and proceeded by boat to Baltimore.

In the night, finding every tavern closed and silent, they walked the remaining forty miles of their journey, tormented by raging thirst, " forced to drink from ditches and standing pools, closing our teeth to keep out the tadpoles and water-beetles." Dusty, footsore, and faint, they trudged along Pennsylvania Avenue, seeking the boarding-house where the member of congress from their district lodged. Taylor always declared that he never recalled that night walk without " a strange reflected sense of pain." The young travelers were presented to Mr. Calhoun, and Taylor felt honored in taking the hand of John Quincy Adams, and hearing a few words of encouragement from his lips. Bayard was the youngest of "the three wise men of Kennett" who were now about to set forth for distant lands. The others were his cousin, Franklin Taylor, and Barclay Pennock. The former had sought out the men of ripest scholarship and strongest personality in New England to study under, and was now going to complete his education in Germany. He became a successful teacher and eloquent lecturer, and president of the Philadelphia Central High School. Pennock is remembered for his Scandinavian studies, and his translation of Keyser's "Religion of the Northmen."

Armed at last with money and with passports, and with light hand-baggage, — "French and German grammars, a portfolio, and a few shirts," — the three friends, at the end of June, 1844, went to New York by the cheapest route, to sail for England. Bayard Taylor called upon N. P. Willis, who received him with gentle courtesy and gave him a letter to his brother, Richard Storrs Willis, who was studying music in Frankfurt, Germany. This interview, from which Bayard Taylor departed with a heart full of gratitude and a mind filled with enthusiasm for his new acquaintance, was an important one in Taylor's life, though he did not yet know it. Willis's hand was to give the genius of Taylor to the literary world. As Taylor expressed a desire to make further engagements with publishers, Willis gave him a general note of introduction — a roving commission — which was calculated to serve his turn and to further his interests with any of the leading journals ; but he was unsuccessful in making more than a conditional engagement with Horace Greeley to furnish sketches of German life and society for the " New York Tribune." In 1844 it was a considerably greater undertaking to cross the ocean than in these times, when we have developed a class of highly civilized beings who keep hopping back and forth across the Atlantic.

In the second cabin of the Oxford, " flanked with bales of cotton and fitted with temporary berths of rough planks," for which accommodation and the privilege of finding their own bedding and provision the travelers paid ten dollars apiece, they left New York on the 1st of July, bound for Liverpool. On the 26th, at sunrise, the Old World dawned upon their view. Taylor gazed with keen excitement upon the scenes his earliest dreams had dwelt upon. His enthusiasm he cast in incoherent words into his diary and his letters. Soon he would enjoy the loveliness that is in English scenery,

and the sweetness that is in English civilization. This first trip to Europe meant so much
for him that it demands recognition in however brief a biography. For him it was no
heedless scamper across a continent, nor guide-
book pilgrimage to cathedrals and castles. It
was no midsummer holiday minted in a golden
mood. It was his university education. For
two years he wandered, " a pensive but unwearied pilgrim," through the lands of Europe,
augmenting his experience and his knowledge
in art galleries and in streets, and reveling in
what of culture was accessible to him with an
intensity of delight of which no thorny point of
penury and sheer distress could rob him.

Instead of going directly to London the travelers made an excursion to the Giants' Cause-
way, and then went from Port Rush to Green-
ock for a run through Scotland. They climbed
Ben Lomond and were present at Ayr on the
occasion of the Burns festival, and saw the sons
of Burns, Professor Wilson, Alison the historian, and Mrs. S. C. Hall. In London Taylor
at first found lodgings in Whitechapel — bare
rooms and questionable beds — for a shilling
a day, but soon shifted his quarters to the Aldgate coffee-house, " where the terms were equally
cheap and the society a very little better."
After a week of sightseeing, in which he made

not a single acquaintance, he left London, and crossed from Dover to Ostend. He journeyed by *Treckshuyt* in Belgium, boated up the Rhine, and walked through the Odenwald.

Frank Taylor meant to study at Heidelberg, and when he registered there for the winter semester Bayard sought Richard Storrs Willis in Frankfurt and there abode six months in snug domestic German quarters. It was a fortunate time for both cousins, for the exodus of the liberals from Göttingen had reinforced Heidelberg with Gervinus and Schlosser, and Bayard, by his residence in a plain burgher family where English was an unknown tongue, made the best possible beginning in the study of the language in which his most notable intellectual triumphs were to be gained. Before the half year was over he was not only fluent in conversation but had written rhyming German verse. Living was cheap. Taylor paid for his furnished rooms, meals, light, and fuel, thirty-three cents a day. Richard Storrs Willis has written pleasantly of Taylor's sojourn with him. In the "Detroit Free Press," May 22, 1887, he says : "Christmas and Thanksgiving, — these of course had to be celebrated by the American colony. Thanksgiving meant a turkey. Where to find one ? It was mortifying to make it clear to our host what we meant by a turkey, — rare in Germany as sweet corn, cranberries, and the oyster.

"As the most enterprising among us, Bayard was deputed to forage among the markets for one. Concealment was vain and he found it. What did he ever seriously undertake and not accomplish? When placed upon the table, our German friends greatly wondered at the unwonted spectacle.

"Christmas meant a gift to our host and hostess. We decided on a carpet for the best company room. Of course we had no carpets on the floor generally; such luxury was confined to the rich, and even then the carpet was mainly a rug. Indeed, after becoming wonted to the cleanly expanse of a floor, a carpet seemed a dusty and untidy thing. We hesitated to dim the whiteness and scrupulous neatness of the floor with it. But we knew it would please our good German friends, and so, after wrestling with the difficulty of choice, innocent of all housekeeping as we were, and just then convinced that a lady comes in very well sometimes (our landlady was out of the question, — it was a Christmas secret), we took the risk of one. Late at night, when all Germans were asleep and only Americans awake, we smuggled the carpet into the room, and like a band of conspirators softly displaced the furniture and surprised the floor with its new adornment.

"Christmas morning, after some quite new

ejaculations on the part of our host and hostess (by which we grammatically profited), we succeeded in overcoming the reluctance to step on it which they at first manifested."

Loyalty to home was one of Taylor's strongest traits. The recollection of the dear homestead at Kennett interposed shadows of melancholy amid the joy and novelty of the life that he was living in the presence of strange beauty and reverend history.

He was entirely ignorant of the ways of the world. Innocent of transgression, true to the cardinal points of heaven and home, the untainted virtue of his years had not yet dived into the world's deceit. By establishing himself in Frankfurt in a simple family where the warm German heart beat with affectionate hospitality he but exchanged home for home. In Kennett his sensibilities had been repressed, his sentimental ardor checked and rebuked. In Frankfurt he experienced the generous glow of gentle sympathies whose effusion, unrestrained by conventions, mellowed his character and liberated his thought. He felt one by one the straitening fetters of old prejudice fall from him, and saw, wide extended before him, the horizon of that untraveled world whose margin fades forever and forever as we move. With fond regret, when he turned away from Frankfurt, he dwelt upon

the scenes now so familiar and so dear, upon the
old bridge with its view up the Main to the far
mountains of the Odenwald, and upon the remembered song of the nightingales heard from
the lovely boulevard ; but Italy was beyond the
mountains, and all the latent love of the beautiful in his nature impelled him toward those
" happy lands " of which Sordello speaks,

> ." That have luxurious names
> For loose fertility ; a footfall there
> Suffices to upturn to the warm air
> Half germinating spices ; mere decay
> Produces richer life; and day by day
> New pollen on the lily-petal grows,
> And still more labyrinthine buds the rose."

It was a long, roundabout way through Germany that he took before descending into Italy.
With a passport, properly viséed, a knapsack
weighing fifteen pounds, and a cane from the
Mammoth Cave of Kentucky, he began a lonely
walk through Northern Germany. He entered
the Hartz, ascended the Brocken in a storm, and
visited Leipsic and Dresden. A brief sojourn
in Prague was followed by a journey through
Bohemia and Moravia, arriving at last at Vienna.
After a few other expeditions and much scrambling among the Alps, he reached Italy by the
passage of the St. Gothard.

In Florence he made his longest stay. His
vague and sensuous delight found permanent ex-

pression many years afterward in " The Picture
of St. John."

> " On, on, through broadening vale and brightening sun
> I walked, and hoary in their old repose
> The olives twinkled : many a terrace rose,
> With marbles crowned and jasmine overrun,
> And orchards where the ivory silk-worm spun.
> On leafy palms outspread, its pulpy fruit
> The fig-tree held ; and last, the charm to close,
> A dark-eyed shepherd piped a reedy flute.

> " My heart beat loud : I walked as in a dream
> Where simplest actions, touched with marvel, seem
> Enchanted yet familiar : for I knew
> The orchards, terraces, and breathing flowers,
> The tree from Adam's garden, and the blue
> Sweet sky behind the light aerial towers ;
> And that young faun that piped, had piped before, —
> I knew my home : the exile now was o'er."

Taylor was too modest to seek the acquaintance of men of note. He had that pearl of virtues, — the capacity for devout veneration, the
sentiment

> " That hallows in the core
> Of human hearts the memory of a wall
> Where dwelt the wise and wondrous," —

and his instant reverence, dearer to him than his
own praise, made him shy of intruding upon the
men whose names he saw shining in the world of
art and letters which it was his dearest ambition to enter. He did seek out Mendelssohn and
Freiligrath, and enjoyed conversation with them.

In Florence he was welcomed by Hiram Powers, in whose house he became acquainted with Richard Adams Locke, the author of the " Moon Hoax." Some verses that Taylor wrote upon Powers' statue of Eve so pleased the sculptor that he procured the author a letter of introduction from Mrs. Trollope to John Murray, her publisher. After borrowing fifty dollars from Mr. Powers, Taylor and his friends found they had just ninety dollars for the journey to Rome and thence to Paris. Taylor had become accustomed to privation. He had known what it was to subsist upon four crazie (six cents) a day, and to live upon bread, figs, and roasted chestnuts. On the 12th of January, 1846, he took deck-passage on a Neapolitan boat from Civita Vecchia for Marseilles. Sick and miserable, lying on the hard deck with a knapsack under his head, wet to the skin, with teeth chattering and limbs numb and damp, Taylor experienced seasickness in all its horrors. Fifteen francs remained upon leaving Marseilles to carry him to Paris. Circumstances now demanded the greatest economy. " The incessant storms of winter and the worn - out state of our shoes, which were no longer proof against water or mud, prolonged our journey considerably, so that by starting before dawn and walking until dark, we were only able to make thirty miles a day." The travelers reached Lyons with clothes like sponges, boots entirely worn out, and bodies suffering from nine days' exposure to the winter storms in a tramp of two hundred and forty miles. They dispatched a letter to Paris requesting that a part of the remittance expected there should be forwarded to Lyons, and they engaged lodgings in a common-looking inn near the river. For five weary, wretched days they lay in pawn, prisoners in Lyons. On the sixth day a letter came — but the postage was fourteen sous, and neither Taylor nor his companion had a centime. By an ingenious manœuvre one of them succeeded in borrowing a franc from the hostess. It required a good deal of courage to break the seal, but then suspense was over, and the remittance was at hand. Forthwith the travelers purchased two delicate cheese-cakes, and in the afternoon new shoes at a small shop in the suburbs. " I gave the cobbler my old pair, which he instantly flung into the street, with the exclamation : ' Ils ne valent pas un sous, Monsieur ! ' " (" Views Afoot," p. 456.)

From Paris Taylor went on to Dieppe and to London. " I stood upon London Bridge, in the raw mist and the falling twilight, with a franc and a half in my pocket, and deliberated what I should do. Weak from seasickness, hungry,

chilled, and without a single acquaintance in the
great city, my situation was about as hopeless
as it is possible to conceive." ("At Home and
Abroad," p. 35.) He sought again the chop-
house opposite the Aldgate Churchyard. His
room contained a miserable bed, an old spinet
with every key broken or out of tune, a cracked
looking-glass, and two chairs. " The window
commanded a cheerful view of the churchyard."
Starvation or downright vagrancy seemed in
store for him, his last penny had gone for bread,
when Mr. Putnam came to his rescue. Every
avenue of employment in London seemed closed
to him by reason of the rules of the English
trade, but Mr. Putnam and Mr. Stevens set him
upon making out catalogues and packing books,
and so for six weeks he earned the scanty sums
that were necessary for his meagre living.

He had brought with him poems which, with
the ignorance and enthusiasm of untried youth,
he believed to be of such a quality as to command the attention of publishers and to create
a sensation in the world of letters. He was
invited by John G. Lockhart to a breakfast
at which he met John Murray and Bernard
Barton. Conversation with the editor of the
" Quarterly Review," and a glimpse into the
old culture and criticism of England, made the
poor little poems in the depths of Taylor's port-

folio, which a short time before had seemed so perfect, look shabby and strange; but it is the best evidence of his sound intellectual health that the discovery brought him no disillusionment and despair, but only, after a night of bitterness and tears, the brave resolve to make his work acceptable to the highest taste and judgment.

On the 1st of June, 1846, the travelers arrived in New York bay and went forward at once to Philadelphia and Wilmington. "Now came the realization of a plan we had talked over a hundred times to keep up our spirits when the weather was gloomy, or the journey lay through some waste of barren country. Our knapsacks, which had been laid down in Paris, were again taken up, slouched German hats substituted for our modern black cylinders, belt and blouse donned, and the pilgrim staff grasped for the rest of our journey. But it was part of our plan that we should not reach home till after nightfall; we could not think of seeing any one we knew before those who were nearest to us; and so it was necessary to wait a few hours before starting.

"The time came; that walk of three or four hours seemed longer than many a day's tramp of thirty miles, but every step of the way was familiar ground. The people we met stared, laughed, or looked suspiciously after us, but we were quite insensible to any observation. We only counted the fields, measured the distance from hill to hill, and watched the gradual decline of the broad bright sun. It went down at last, and our homes were not far off. When the twilight grew deeper, we parted, each one of us thinking what an experience lay between that moment and the next morning. I took to the fields, plunged into a sea of dewy clover, and made for a light which began to glimmer as it grew darker. When I reached it, and looked with the most painful excitement through the window on the unsuspecting group within, there was not one face missing." [1]

Bayard Taylor returned from his eventful journey with rich eyes and poor hands. His mind had been enlarged but his character was unchanged. "He was born," said Berthold Auerbach in his funeral address, "in the New World, but *ripened* in the Old." He had departed a youth, he returned a man. It was on a day of warm sun, of blue sky and bluer sea, that, walking by the Italian shore of the Mediterranean, Bayard Taylor celebrated in thought and thankfulness his twenty-first birthday. He had endured much and suffered much, but his gains were beyond his present audit.

[1] *Views Afoot*, p. 494.

"Who ne'er his bread with sorrow ate,
   Who ne'er the lonely midnight hours
With weeping on his bed hath sate,
   He knows ye not, ye heavenly powers."

When sauntering through the streets of European towns he had frequently attracted much attention, with his student cap and his year's growth of hair. And now he found that at home a lively interest had been awakened in him by the publication of his letters in the " Tribune," " Saturday Evening Post," and " United States Gazette." He was advised to collect his letters and publish them in a book, and for that purpose he went to New York, where he negotiated with Wiley & Putnam, who agreed to pay him one hundred dollars for every thousand copies sold.

Willis suggested the title " Views Afoot," and generously wrote for the book an introduction, " giving," as Taylor in a later edition said, " the buoyancy of his name to a craft which might not otherwise have ridden so fortunately the capricious sea of literary success."

The poetic fervor of the book and its restrained vigor of style, the tenacity of purpose, the struggle, the courage, and the pluck that it revealed, fascinated the public, and sufficiently account for its great popularity. It appeared under the title : " Views Afoot ; or, Europe seen

with Knapsack and Staff. By J. Bayard Taylor, with a preface by N. P. Willis. New York:
Wiley & Putnam, 1846." It was dedicated to
his cousin, Frank Taylor, who had shared the
toils and enjoyments of the pilgrimage. The
manuscript Bayard had submitted to Hannah
Darlington, one of his earliest and most sympathetic friends, and her " critical judgment," he
declared in the copy of the book that he presented to her, " assisted in polishing and preparing " it.

Six editions were sold in the first year. A
chapter of practical hints to pedestrians was
added to the eighth edition. The twentieth
edition appeared in 1855, and it was marked
by a thorough revision and a new introductory
chapter.

Longfellow wrote of it, under date of Christmas Day, 1846 : " The last chapter fills me
with great wonder. How could you accomplish
so much, with such slight help and appliances?
It shows a strength of will — the central fire of
all great deeds and words — that must lead you
far in whatever you undertake."

He received kind letters of appreciation from
Mary Howitt, Eliza Leslie, Mrs. Hale, and Bernard Barton ; and Friedrich Gerstäcker wrote
from Germany to interest him in one of the in-
terminable American novels that he was then

writing, — perhaps " Die Flusspiraten des Mis-
sissippi."

Horace Greeley recalling his early employment of Taylor wrote : " I say, then, most earn-
estly, to every youth anxious to go abroad,
traverse Europe, and pay his way by writing
for some journal, ' Tarry at Jericho, till your
beard be grown.' I never knew but one of
your class — Bayard Taylor — who achieved a
real success in thus traveling ; and he left home
a good type-setter, with some knowledge of modern languages ; so that he stopped and worked
at his trade whenever his funds ran short ; yet,
even thus, he did not wholly pay his way during the two years he devoted to his delightful
' Views Afoot.' I know it, for I employed and
paid him all that his letters were fairly worth,
though not nearly so much as his letters *now*
righteously command. He practiced a syste-
matic and careful economy ; yet he went away
with money, and returned with the clothes on
his back, and (I judge) very little more. My
young friend, if you think yourself better quali-
fied than he was, go ahead, and ' do ' Europe !
but don't ask me to further your scheme ; for I
hold that you may far better stay at home, ap-
ply yourself to some useful branch of produc-
tive industry, help pay our national debt, and
accumulate a little independence whereon, by

and by, to travel (if you choose) as a gentleman, and not with but a sheet of paper between
you and starvation." [1]

Almost at the same time with the approval of
his prose, came the first praise of his poetry.
In the winter of 1846–47 he published anonymously " The Norseman's Ride," in the " Dem-
ocratic Review."   Whittier read it, and copied
it into the " National Era," prefacing it with
commendation.   Taylor wrote to him from
Phœnixville under date of September 16, 1847 :

" I know you will understand the feeling which
prompts me, though a stranger, to address you,
and pardon any liberties I may have taken in
so doing.   I was surprised and delighted a few
weeks ago to see in the 'National Era,' in connection with a notice of the old northern mythology, a poem of mine, ' The Norseman's Ride,'
which was published last winter in the 'Demo-
cratic Review.'   I am an enthusiastic admirer of
the stirring Scandinavian sagas, some of which
Tegnér has immortalized in his 'Frithiof;' and
it was under the full influence of the spirit inspired by them that the poem was written.   I
was *possessed* by the subject and fancied I had
given it fitting expression, but the friends to
whom I showed it did not admire it, and I re-

[1] Horace Greeley, *Recollections of a Busy Life*, p. 326.

luctantly concluded that my heated fancies had led my judgment astray, and made up my mind to forget it. Judge, then, how grateful and encouraging was your generous commendation. I thank you sincerely and from my heart for the confidence your words have given me. One day, I hope, I shall be able to take your hand, and tell you what happiness it is to be understood by one whom the world calls by the sacred name of poet. With every wish for your happiness and prosperity, I am, with sincere respect and esteem, your friend, J. BAYARD TAYLOR."[1]

Three years later Whittier reviewed "Eldorado" in the "National Era," and suggested to Taylor that he would find a promising field of travel "in the vast territory of New Mexico, — the valley of the Del Norte, with its old Castilian and Aztec monuments and associations; the Great Salt Lake, and the unexplored regions of the great valley of Colorado, between the mountain ranges of the Sierra Madre and the Sierra Nevada." Taylor replied: "If it was not time that I should stop from roving and build up a home for myself, I would go there next year."

The friendship so knit grew in love and loyalty. Taylor's visits to Amesbury Whittier has referred to in "The Last Walk in Autumn."

[1] Pickard's *Whittier*, vol. i. pp. 325, 326.

> " Here, too, of answering love secure
> 　　Have I not welcomed to my hearth
> 　　The gentle pilgrim Troubadour,
> 　　Whose songs have girdled half the earth;
> 　　Whose pages, like the magic mat
> 　　Whereon the Eastern lover sat,
> Have borne me over Rhineland's purple vines
> And Nubia's tawny sands, and Phrygia's mountain pines."

In " The Tent on the Beach " Whittier brings together three congenial companions within sound of the bells of Newburyport, and listens to the stories that they tell. Whittier and James T. Fields are two of the company ; the other, —

> " One whose Arab face was tanned
> 　　By tropic sun and boreal frost,
> 　　So traveled there was scarce a land
> 　　Or people left him to exhaust,
> 　　In idling mood had from him hurled
> 　　The poor squeezed orange of the world,
> And in the tent-shade, as beneath a palm,
> Smoked, cross-legged like a Turk, in Oriental calm.

> " His memory round the ransacked earth
> 　　On Ariel's girdle slid at ease ;
> 　　And, instant, to the valley's girth
> 　　Of mountains, spice isles of the seas,
> 　　Faith flowered in minster stones, Art's guess
> 　　At truth and beauty, found access ;
> Yet loved the while, that free cosmopolite,
> Old friends, old ways, and kept his boyhood's dreams in sight."

In this " free cosmopolite," merrily chatting with his friends, and improvising song

and story, there must be instant recognition
of the far-traveled Pennsylvanian poet, who
in his turn gave Whittier verse for verse by
dedicating to him " Lars : A Pastoral of Norway."

> " Through many years my heart goes back,
>   Through checkered years of loss and gain,
>   To that fair landmark on its track,
>   When first, beside the Merrimack,
> Upon thy cottage roof I heard the autumn rain."

Soon after the publication of " Views Afoot "
Taylor visited Boston, and was feasted and
praised by Whipple and Fields, and presented
by them to Longfellow. He blushed at the
general chorus of compliment and congratulation, and wept for sheer excitement and for joy.
And now he looked about him for some occupation that would yield him a fixed income. He
weighed the chances in country journalism, and,
reflecting that the neighboring counties, Chester
and Montgomery, supported seven political papers, believed that there was a field for a periodical devoted to literature and news. Dr. I. A.
Pennypacker recommended Phœnixville as the
place of publication. A paper already located
there, the " Phœnixville Gazette," was bought
by Taylor and his friend Frederick E. Foster,
and, its name being changed, was issued December 29, 1846, as the "Phœnixville Pioneer."

Taylor wrote most of the editorials and all of the book reviews.

Phœnixville was a manufacturing place, resounding with the roar of forges, and brilliant at night with columns of red flame rising from the mills and furnaces. The chief laboring class had no interest in the aims of the "Pioneer." The farmers with rustic conservatism regarded the town with dislike and the paper with disfavor. Taylor worked faithfully at his task, sped the nights with poetry and translation, resumed his habit of pedestrianism, rowed in the afternoons upon French Creek, and joined spiritedly in the diversions of the town's small society of educated persons. That he viewed the slow progress of the journal with ill-concealed discontent was due neither to ambition nor chagrin, but to deep disappointment at his inability to compass what was then the one darling purpose of his life. He had not breathed it in his letters, he had scarcely confided it to his diary, he had not whispered to a friend the pure affection for one who was the purest and gentlest of women, that had grown with his growth and had become the precious ideal of his life. His mother alone possessed the secret. When he went abroad in 1844 the sorest pang was parting from the one who held his heart in keeping; and the image of that sweet face lived

with him in his wanderings. Thirteen years
before his memorable voyage, when he was a
child at the dame's school, Mary Agnew, a little
neighbor and schoolmate whom he loved, whispered to the teacher, "May I sit beside Bayard?" The same dear companion was in his
mind when he gave with mingled fear and pride
his first volume of poems to the press.

Upon his return to Kennett, his engagement
became known. It is a rarely beautiful personality that is disclosed in the letters of Mary
Agnew as published in the "Life and Letters
of Bayard Taylor." Grace Greenwood once described her as "a dark-eyed young girl with the
rose yet unblighted on cheek and lip, with soft,
brown, wavy hair, which, when blown by the
wind, looked like the hair often given to angels
by the old masters, producing a sort of halo-like
effect about a lovely head." It was to provide
a home for her that Bayard was straining every
energy, but the present still seemed hopeless
and the future was veiled in impenetrable clouds.

A brief run to the Catskills in August gave
him another teasing glimpse of metropolitan life
in New York. After his return to Phœnixville
he wrote to Willis for information about New
York journalism, and received from him the
advice to negotiate by correspondence with certain editors of the city before abandoning his

business in the country. In reply to the letters
that he addressed to the men whom he best
knew, Greeley wrote dissuading him from the
venture ; Griswold, with his usual sanguine
temper, had no hesitation in bidding him come
at once ; Bryant knew of no vacancy ; Charles
Fenno Hoffman liked his idea of " ' coming up
to the capital,' as did the worthies of literature
in Johnson's time," and offered him an engagement for November and December at five dollars
a week upon the miscellaneous department of
the " Literary World."

Bayard Taylor now took the second decisive
step of his life. He had wasted a year in un-
profitable toil. He had incurred what was to
him a serious burden of debt. He now bought
his release from the partnership in the " Pioneer,"
and arrived in New York, December 17, 1847.
He was engaged by Hoffman at five dollars a
week, and he had an offer from Miss Green to
teach *belles-lettres* at her school, three or four
hours a week, for four dollars more.

He was in the metropolis, and he was on the
threshold of his fame.

CHAPTER II.

1848–1853.

BAYARD TAYLOR'S intellectual development was never steadily progressive. What he lacked in originality he supplied by eager industry. To get from him the best of which he was capable it was necessary for him to feel strong external stimulus. Throngs of men and urgent competition summoned into activity all his energies and capabilities. He adapted himself to all circumstances and surroundings; he bore apparently without fatigue the labors that bowed and crushed other men of less heroic strength. When a definite task was given him to discharge and rival intellects raced with him in the performance of it, his surprising alertness of mind, unfailing physical health, and astonishing industry of hand assured him a victory that was always secure and sometimes brilliant.

His career, therefore, resolves itself into clearly marked epochs corresponding to certain influences entering accidentally or otherwise into his life. The year at Phœnixville had been full of restless pain; Pegasus was restive in rustic harness. The removal to New York, by introducing Taylor to the best and busiest literary life of the country, afforded scope for his ambition, and gave direction to his vague and wandering aspirations. The time, too, was propitious. Philadelphia had entirely lost her old supremacy as the capital city of American letters.

The satirist Duganne, who was for a time associated with the publication of the " Iron Man," a paper which, after Taylor's " Pioneer " had ceased, continued a short and uneventful existence in Phœnixville during 1849 and 1850, said what every writer knew to be the fact, —

> " Yet true it is, and that 't is true, 't is pity,
> The pen is penury in Penn's great city." [1]

Nothing is more patent to the patient reader of the Philadelphia periodicals from 1820 to 1840 than the swift progress of New York beyond the Pennsylvanian city. With the passing of Brown and Dennie, and the literary clique that had supported the " Port-Folio," there arose in New York a new group of writers, having few features in common, but conveniently labeled " the Knickerbocker school." A. J. H.

[1] *Parnassus in Pillory*, a satire, by Motley Manners, Esq. New York, 1851.

Duganne in "Parnassus in Pillory" lampooned
the American authors, and in his eagerness to
castigate Willis referred ironically to his kindly
care of Bayard Taylor : —

> "What time Nat Willis, in the daily papers,
>   Published receipts of shoemakers and drapers:
> What time, in sooth, his 'Mirror' flashed its rays,
>   Like Barnum's 'drummond,' on the Broadway gaze ;[1]
> When lisping misses, fresh from seminaries,
>   Worshiped 'mi-boy' and 'brigadier'[2] as *lares;*
> Then Bayard Taylor — protégé of Natty,
>   Dixon-like[3] walked into the 'literati'!
> And first to proper use his genius put,
>   Like ballet-girls, by showing 'Views Afoot.'"

New York had already assumed a cosmopolitan
and commercial character, and there was about
it a lively and extravagant tone which contrasted
strikingly with the seriousness of Boston and
the provincialism of Philadelphia. That Taylor
was delighted with the swifter currents of metropolitan life is evident from his letters to Kennett Square. When he meditated a removal
to Philadelphia to work for Mr. Graham, he
wrote to Mary Agnew (May 11, 1846): "How
shall I leave this mighty New York? I cannot
think it will be a final departure. Something

[1] The office of the *Mirror* was near Barnum's Museum, and
the Drummond light.

[2] Willis and Morris signed their articles "Mi-boy," and
"Brigadier."

[3] George Washington Dixon, "literary-musical-pedestrian."

tells me that a great part of my destiny shall be worked out here. It is almost the only place in this country where the mind can grow without restriction. Philadelphia is merely an immense provincial town ; *here* is the metropolis of a continent ! "

The opinion formed upon the first encounter with the literary workers of New York, Taylor never found cause to change. Many years later he wrote to Prof. James Morgan Hart, to whom he was indebted for judicious criticism of his translation of " Faust," " I wish you could have settled in New York rather than in Boston. The intellectual tone is *higher* in the latter place, but *freer* in the former. Besides New York is in the process of evolution in a literary sense, which Boston does not seem to be : in other words there is rather more of a future in our noisy metropolis."

At the moment when Taylor " walked into the ' literati,' " Bryant, Halleck, and Willis were the most prominent men of letters ; and all of them were native New Englanders. Halleck had counted the Muse's children in New York many years before, and found that

> " Our fourteen wards
> Contain some thirty-seven bards."

Washington Irving had freshly returned from Spain and taken up his residence at Sunnyside, the "pretty little cabin," as Thackeray called it, at Tarrytown; Taylor met him, and found him "a glorious old man, full of kind, genial feelings, and most delightful in his conversation."

James Fenimore Cooper was living in the old hall on Lake Otsego with three years of authorship still before him. James Kirke Paulding had practically closed his literary career, — although "The Puritan and His Daughter," the last of his novels, was still unpublished, — and had retired to "Placentia," his beautiful home upon the Hudson. General George P. Morris was occupying his summer home, "Undercliff," opposite to West Point; and Willis, who had not yet acquired the estate upon the Hudson near Newburgh which, with his customary felicity, he named "Idlewild," was the best-dressed figure upon Broadway.

Charles Fenno Hoffman, who was the first editor of the "Knickerbocker Magazine," and who wrote "Monterey," a favorite poem with General Grant, and the still popular song, "Sparkling and Bright," had already begun to show slight symptoms of the malady which issued in hopeless insanity. Hoffman's boarding-house, Murray Street, near Broadway, became Bayard Taylor's first residence in New York, and Taylor was fascinated by the glitter of his

companion's eccentric fancy, and counted himself happy in his acquaintance. The year before Taylor appeared in New York, Verplanck
had published his edition of Shakespeare, with
notes, and the Duyckinck brothers had begun
" The Literary World." It was the fashion to
compare our writers with the English favorites
of the hour: Hoffman was our Knickerbocker
Moore, Halleck was supposed to suggest Campbell. Imitation was the life and breath of the
Knickerbocker literature, and it is perhaps not
unfair to conclude, with J. K. Dennett ("Nation," December 5, 1867), that "it is true to
say that the Knickerbocker school was composed
of authors whom we all remember as forgotten." Taylor was quickly made free of the social
life of New York through the courtesy of his
mentor, Willis, and his house-mate, Hoffman.
On New Year's night, 1848, he attended a *con-
versazione* at Anne Lynch's (Mrs. Botta) whose
parlors once a week for nearly half a century
were hospitably open to the guilds of art and
letters. Hoffman introduced him to the society
that gathered around Mrs. Seba Smith, the
wife of " Major Jack Downing," in Brooklyn.
Much of sentimentalism and affectation, of
course, there was in some of the pseudo-liter-
ary gatherings. In " John Godfrey's Fortunes "
Taylor satirizes the receptions of those fantastics

who had "only got the tune of the time and
outward habit of encounter;" no doubt there
were many unconventional "at homes" like
Adeliza Choate's Friday nights when similar
"fond and winnowed opinions" were idly discussed. Lest the sarcasm in the description
might be interpreted wrongly, Taylor wrote, —
with Miss Lynch's *conversaziones* in his mind,
— "The Friday evening receptions of Mrs.
Yorkton — I beg pardon, Adeliza Choate —
continued to be given, but I did not often attend
them. I had been fortunate enough to obtain
entrance to the literary *soirées* of another lady
whom I will not name, but whose tact, true
refinement of character, and admirable culture
drew around her all that was best in letters and
in the arts. In her *salons* I saw the possessors
of honored and illustrious names; I heard books
and pictures discussed with the calm discrimi-
nation of intelligent criticism; the petty vanities
and jealousies I had hitherto encountered might
still exist, but they had no voice, and I soon
perceived the difference between those who aspire and those who achieve. Art, I saw, has its
own peculiar microcosm, — its born nobles, its
plodding, conscientious, respectable middle class,
and its clamorous, fighting rabble." ("John
Godfrey's Fortunes," p. 321.)

Occasional social diversion **and the** writing

of poetical valentines and humorous acrostics did not interfere with the rapid dispatch of thorough work. Greeley was so impressed by Taylor's energy and enthusiasm that before the end of January, 1848, he offered him a situation on the "Tribune." Oliver Johnson had resigned, and the miscellaneous and literary department was without a chief. To this post Taylor was appointed, at a salary of twelve dollars a week, at a time when the town was full of five-dollars-a-week men, and when it was necessary to work for several papers in order to earn enough to keep life afoot. "I seem to have turned over a new leaf of life," wrote Taylor to Mary Agnew, "and I shall write a better story upon it than the blotted pages I have left behind."

In "John Godfrey's Fortunes" Taylor refers with pleasant humor to his first experiences in city journalism, and to his rapture and gratitude at what he calls a "branch of Pactolus bursting at my feet to bear me onward to all golden possibilities." His work and manner attracted almost instant attention, and the stranger who had been introduced to New York by N. P. Willis in January, received in the first week of March invitations to four additional situations. Mrs. Kirkland was going to Europe and would have Taylor edit "The Union

Magazine " and " Christian Inquirer " until her
return; George R. Graham, always quick to dis-
cern new talent, engaged him to write occasional
book reviews; and Henry Peterson, author of
" Pemberton," asked him to become the New
York correspondent of the " Saturday Evening
Post." In July one of the owners of " Graham's
Magazine " waited upon Taylor and offered him
the permanent editorship of that periodical at a
thousand dollars a year, but this prize he was
not destined to possess; the affairs of " Graham's
Magazine," which had been disordered finan-
cially, were adjusted, and Bayard Taylor continued to hold a merely nominal editorship, and to
furnish regular contributions without leaving
New York. So quickly did his reputation kindle
before him that in December, 1848, James T.
Fields wrote to him, " You have a capital reputation now in poetry, and must be careful of
your muse. A good beginning is everything.
I stand at a desk where I can gauge a man's
depth in the public reading estimation, and I
know no youngster who stands dearer than J.
B. T., doffing the J." The last words of the
letter contained sensible advice. The " J." was
the Mordecai at the gate of a good and poetic
name.

Bayard Taylor's excitement during this busy
year was intense. He reveled in the delight of

the intellect. To no kind of newspaper duty
was he averse; book notices, editorials, domestic news, foreign intelligence, reporter's notes,
fell profusely from his untiring and always careful hand. He wrote fifteen hours a day; and
in his rooms at an aerial elevation, "o'erlooking
the city's tiles," he wrote late into the night, or
ran a swift race before the dawn, "resting his
soul with poetry after the prosaic labors of the
day." The vivid sensations created by the romance of the West as it appeared in the daily
news from the gold-fields, stimulated him to the
making of the "Californian Ballads," — poems
that are spangled with such beauty as only
youthful passion can bestow.

The friendships that are formed in the ideal-
izing time of generous youth are the most potent
and most permanent. To the romantic attach-
ments formed by poets in their youth we often
owe the direction and the profit of their lives.
Such a friendship bound together the lives of
Bayard Taylor and Richard Henry Stoddard.
Separated during the week by sharp necessity,
Taylor performing his round of journalistic
duty, and Stoddard leaving many "weary prints
on the wet sands of a hated foundry," they met
on Saturday nights to enjoy what Taylor called

> "The sunshine of the Gods,
> The hour of perfect Song."

To one another they dedicated their books. When Taylor wrote " Ariel in the Cloven Pine-Tree," Stoddard companioned it with " Caliban, the Witch's Whelp," and when a great sorrow fell upon Stoddard and his noble wife, it was Bayard Taylor who spoke the gentlest sympathy, and sweetly recalled

> " The finer soul, that unto ours
>   A subtle perfume seemed to be,
> Like incense blown from April flowers
>   Beside the scarred and stormy tree." [1]

" I have before me now," writes Mr. Stoddard, " a vision of him [Taylor] in his young manhood, — tall, erect, active looking, and manly, with an aquiline nose, bright, loving eyes, and the dark, ringleted hair with which we endow, in ideal, the head of poets. There was a kindness and a courtesy in his greeting which went straight to my heart, and assured me that I had found a friend."

Stoddard followed Keats, and Taylor studied Shelley. The revolutionary spirits of both the English poets lived in the quick pulses of their worshipers. Their sensuous beauty, their subtle harmonies, and their lofty imagination tortured the young imitators with exquisite delight and with despair. An " Ode to Shelley " was the best poem, with the possible exception of

---

[1] *Euphorion.*

" The Continents," — praised by Poe, — that Taylor composed in 1848.

When time had tried and proved the friendship that had ennobled their youth, Taylor addressed to Mr. Stoddard the sonnet: —

TO R. H. S.

The years go by, old Friend ! Each, as it fleets,
Moves to a farther, fairer realm, the time
When first we twain the pleasant land of Rhyme
Discovered, choosing side by side our seats
Below our separate Gods : in midnight streets
And haunted attics flattered by the chime
Of silver words, and, fed by faith sublime,
I Shelley's mantle wore, you that of Keats, —
Dear dreams, that marked the Muse's childhood then,
Nor now to be disowned ! The years go by ;
The clear-eyed Goddess flatters us no more ;
And yet, I think, in soberer aims of men,
And Song's severer service, you and I
Are nearer, dearer, faithfuller than before.

Another poet was, in this year (1848), admitted to wear with these the muse's livery. One of Taylor's earliest literary duties had been to review " The Lesson of Life, and other Poems," and to abuse the book. Six weeks after he had obeyed the order he became acquainted with the author, explained the review, and apologized for the fault. Then and there began a close and unfaltering friendship between Bayard Taylor and George Henry Boker. A "Sonnet to G. H. B." expresses Taylor's appreciation of

Boker's genius, as well as his love for the man : —

> " If that my hand, like yours, dear George, were skilled
>   To win from Wordsworth's scanty plot of ground
>   A stirring harvest, such as you have found,
>   Where strength and grace, fraternally fulfilled,
>   As in those sheaves whose rustling glories gild
>   The hills of August, folded are, and bound ;
>   So would I draw my loving tillage round
>   Its borders, bid the gentlest rains be spilled,
>   The goldenest suns its happy growth compel,
>   And bind for you the ripe, redundant grain :
>   But, ah, you stand amid your songful sheaves,
>   So rich, this weed-born flower you might disdain,
>   Save that of me its growth and color tell,
>   And of my love some perfume haunt its leaves ! "

The fourth member of the "tuneful quire," and always a welcome visitor when fortune brought him to New York, was T. Buchanan Read. Both his arts, painting and poetry, were made to express the love and friendship he bore his comrades. He painted a picture, in the sentimental style prevailing in the "forties," of Taylor, a slender youth, of Shelley's face and form, equipped with palmer's hat and blouse, and a shepherd's crook doing duty for the nonce as an alpenstock. In the background hills peep o'er hills, and Alps on Alps arise.

In poetry Read has depicted Taylor in the character of Arthur in the "Home Pastorals." Some years later (1855) Taylor found an-

other friend in Thomas Bailey Aldrich, with
whom he exchanged poetic confidences, and from
whom he gained valuable suggestions and learned
profitable lessons. The best poem upon the
death of Taylor was Aldrich's, and the heartiest
sonnet that Taylor ever wrote was on Aldrich's
wedding.

TO T. B. A. AND L. W.

Sad Autumn, drop thy weedy crown forlorn,
Put off thy cloak of cloud, thy scarf of mist,
And dress in gauzy gold and amethyst
A day benign, of sunniest influence born,
As may befit a Poet's marriage morn!
Give buds another dream, another tryst
To loving hearts, and print on lips unkissed
Betrothal kisses, laughing Spring to scorn!
Yet if unfriendly thou, with sullen skies,
Bleak rains, or moaning winds, dost menace wrong,
Here art thou foiled : a bridal sun shall rise
And bridal emblems unto these belong.
Round her the sunshine of her beauty lies,
And breathes round him the Spring-time of his song!

Taylor grew rapidly in knowledge of literature, and acquaintance with literary men. He
heard Richard Henry Dana, who was lecturing
in New York, in 1848, on old English Literature, and was thereby led to the study of the
ballads, the dramatists, and Wordsworth. Many
years later (1875) Taylor was sitting with Dana
in his home upon the New England coast, and
asked him if the spirit of Lee ever rode the

waters below him. Dana replied, "Twenty years ago, or more, the body of a horse was washed ashore here, and it happened to be a *white* horse."

While Taylor was editing Mrs. Kirkland's "Union Magazine," Greeley came to him with a roll of manuscript and said, "Now you must do something for this young man. His name is Thoreau. He lives in a shanty at Walden Pond, near Concord, on $37.21 a year, and he must be encouraged." The manuscript was "Katahdin [which Thoreau spelled Ktaadn] and the Maine Woods." Taylor persuaded the publisher to give seventy-five dollars for it, but the good that he meant to do he did not do, for when the article appeared the shocking misprint of "scows" for "æons" in a cosmical phrase about the development of man's nautical genius drew Thoreau's indignation down upon Taylor's editorial head.

His responsibility for the "Union Magazine" ceased in September, 1848, and in the following month he widened his circle of literary acquaintanceship by a visit to New England which gave him an evening with Lowell, a night with Longfellow, a ramble with Whittier, and an opportunity to report for the "Tribune" one of Webster's speeches delivered in the pine woods of Abington. He discharged all the miscellaneous duties of a newspaper reporter, was with Willis and Griswold and Lewis Gaylord Clark on the first train which crossed the Cascade Ravine bridge, and reported with vividness and precision the frenzy of the Astor Place riots. The terrible night of the tenth of May, 1849, and the military encampments in the street for the three succeeding nights kindled Taylor's excitement, and the accounts in the " Tribune" are equaled only by the circumstantial report furnished by Mr. Bangs to the " Sunday Courier." By this time Taylor had been advanced upon the " Tribune " and had become a stockholder in the company.

It was just at the close of the " roaring forties " that the contagion of the " gold fever " spread from California across the Continent. Torrents of miscellaneous emigration set westward, and a strange and extraordinary life began upon the Pacific slope. Of that wild life, " replete with a certain Greek heroism," with its lapses into semi-savagery, its sudden passions, and its moral romances, we have nowhere a more accurate or more cheerful picture than in Taylor's letters to the " Tribune." His fame as a traveler and his skill as a reporter were already such that he was chosen without hesitation as the likeliest man to accomplish the perilous and peculiar task of describing the situation in Cal-

ifornia as it really was. He was exactly of the
mood and temper to appreciate what he saw in
the young community. " Eager-hearted as a boy
when first he leaves his father's field," he heard
his days before him and the tumult of his life.
Full of health and hope, eager of heart and eye,
he was all aglow with the enthusiasm of the
great scenes before him. Discomforts and hin-
drances were no impediment or discouragement
to him. Even of the dreadful journey across the
isthmus, a terror to emigrants, he says, " I feel
fresh enough to turn about and make the trip
over again." He sailed for California June 28,
1849, and thus summarizes his journey : " I went
by way of the Isthmus of Panama, — the route
had just been opened, — reached San Francisco
in August, and spent five months in the midst of
the rough, half-savage life of a new country. I
lived almost entirely in the open air, sleeping on
the ground with my saddle for a pillow, and
sharing the hardships of the gold-diggers without taking part in their labors. Returning
through Mexico, which I traversed diagonally
from Mazatlan to Vera Cruz, I reached New
York in March, 1850, and resumed my duties as
editor." In the month of his return the record
of his travel and its observations appeared under
the title, " Eldorado, or Adventures in the Path
of Empire ; comprising a Voyage to California,

via Panama ; Life in San Francisco and Monterey ; Pictures of the Gold Region, and Experiences of Mexican Travel."

No more optimistic view of the life in the mining camps was ever taken. Crime and distress made no lasting impression upon Taylor. " He saw whatever illustrated life, hope, vigor, courage, prosperity." [1] His pages are strewn with such favorable comments as, " There was as much security to life and property as in any part of the Union, and as small a proportion of crime ; " and again, " The cosmopolitan cast of society in California, resulting from the commingling of so many races and the primitive mode of life, gave a character of good fellowship to all its members."

The colossal features of Western scenery fascinated Taylor's imagination. He continually digressed into descriptions that fell little short of poetic rapture. He writes : " The broad oval valleys shaded by magnificent oaks, and enclosed by the lofty mountains of the Coast Range, open beyond each other like a suite of parlor chambers, each charming more than the last ! " In a letter to Mary Agnew he writes : " It is so delicious to fall asleep with the stars above you, — to feel their rays, the last thing glimmering in your hazy consciousness, and then shining on,

[1] Josiah Royce, *California*, p. 304.

brighter and purer, in your dreams! How often under the sycamores or evergreen oaks, with my head on a dragoon saddle and a Mexican blanket rolled warmly around me, have I lain in the silent wilderness, and thought of thee! One night which I will tell thee of when we meet, I slept, or rather watched, all alone on the top of a mountain, with vast plains glimmering in the moonlight below me and the wolves howling far down in the ravines. Was it not a glorious night?" That "top of a mountain" is so like Taylor. He was fond of great heights and broad views; and the child who astonished the servant-girl with the discovery of the Falls of Niagara from his perilous station upon the comb of the steep roof of his Kennett home, was father of the traveler who stood upon the high places of the world and took in the widest sweep of vision in the five continents.

After an experience with robbers in Mexico, he reached New York, March 9, 1850. His salary upon the "Tribune" was increased, and he was the owner of three shares of its stock, but the joy of success and the delight of advancement were painfully checked by the apprehension at Kennett. Mary Agnew became ill in April with inflammation of the lungs, and from the effects of that malady she never recovered. The wedding, which had been set for

June 19th, was indefinitely postponed. Taylor performed his many tasks with his customary alacrity and thoroughness, but back of all his industry and apparent eagerness was a constant agony of grief, and the haunting fear of the loss of the dearest object upon earth to him, and the fall at once of all the high built projects of his life.

City items, California news, Cuban expeditions, and such bubbles of the moment did not alone fill up his worried days. Upon the invitation early in May of the Phi Beta Kappa Society of Harvard College, he set about composing a poem, "The American Legend," to be read at Commencement in July. It was received with marked favor; Emerson pronounced it the best poem which had ever been delivered there. Taylor was elected an honorary member of the Φ B K Society. He received the congratulations of Felton and Dana and Lowell, and with Lowell started the next day for Amesbury to spend a long day with Whittier. Invitations enough descended upon him to furnish him, as he said, " with two weeks' board." But declining all inducements to stay he returned to New York on Sunday morning, July 21, and the next day was summoned to Fire Island to the scene of the shipwreck of the Elizabeth. The American Sibyl, Margaret Fuller, with her Italian husband, the Marquis d'Ossoli, and her child, and Horace Sumner (brother of Charles), after the failure of the Revolution of 1848 embarked at Leghorn on the merchant vessel Elizabeth for New York. After a succession of mishaps the gale that arose as they approached the American coast strengthened into a hurricane that shattered the Elizabeth to fragments upon Fire Island. For a week Taylor lingered at the scene of the wreck, whither Charles Sumner and Henry D. Thoreau had come. Neither Margaret Fuller nor her husband was found, and the manuscript of the " Revolutions in Italy " was lost with them.

Free for a breathing-space from imperative engagements, Taylor hastened to Kennett, whence had come alarming reports of Mary Agnew's condition. In the thought that a change of air and scene might be beneficial, she was brought by her mother and by Bayard to Philadelphia for medical consultation, and then taken to West Point. It soon became necessary to seek a more quiet resort, and this was found at the farmhouse of a Mrs. Sutherland at Cornwall, in the highlands of the Hudson, a place where the Willises were staying and which subsequently became their home and known to the world as Idlewild. A fortnight the ladies remained at this quiet, secluded spot,

and then returned to Kennett warned by the
sudden and chill approach of autumn. Mary
Agnew seemed improved in health, her cough
was less frequent and exhausting, and her
strength appeared to be returning. These were
the delusive symptoms most common in mala-
dies like hers, but they thrilled Bayard Taylor
with fresh hope and devotion, and at his desk
in New York, bowed over the miscellaneous
tasks of the newspaper office, he worked with
a more resolute pen, and cast about him upon
every side for the means to make possible and
prosperous his married life, which was now his
one engrossing object.

When the Muses declare a competition there
is usually an astonishing revelation in the most
unlooked for places of the numerical force of
their worshipers. It is much easier to imitate
emotion than is popularly supposed. The little
ripple of laughter evoked by Mr. Douglas
Sladen's "One Hundred Bards of America"
was unreasonable, for that cunning hunter of
"mute inglorious Miltons" might have many
times multiplied his list, and still have omitted
some easy versifiers who are covetous of the
poet's name. An enterprising Western pub-
lishing house has given the biographies and
portraits of more than twelve hundred "poets
of America" and by no means exhausted the

singing choir. In the autumn of 1850 P. T.
Barnum, the incomparable showman, who had
contracted with Jenny Lind to sing for one hundred and fifty nights in America, offered two
hundred dollars as a prize for an original song
for the "Swedish Nightingale." "All the versifiers in the land," says Stoddard, "set at
once to work to immortalize themselves and to
better their fortunes, and as many as six hundred confidently expected to do so."[1] The committee appointed to decide among the jarring
claimants of the prize selected two of the contributions, and, unable or unwilling to choose between them, submitted both to Jenny Lind, who
chose the shorter and more patriotic, which was
Taylor's. Then broke forth the high clangor-
ous rage of the whole *irritabile genus;* Taylor was dubbed "Barnum's poet-laureate;"
he was adjudged the winner because his publisher, Mr. Putnam, and his fellow-editor on the
"Tribune," Mr. Ripley, were of the committee.
Newspaper offices were besieged by wild-eyed
poets bearing their verses with them as conspicuous evidence of their superior rights to the
prize and the glory. The papers teemed for a
while with every variety of "rejected addresses,"
"from an epigram up to an epic."

[1] Taylor says there were 752 disappointed candidates.
[Letter to Mary Agnew, September 18, 1850.]

Bayard Taylor's unfortunately successful lyric was set to music by Jules Benedict and was sung by Jenny Lind at her first concert in Castle Garden.

To be abused was a new sensation to Bayard Taylor, and his correspondence at this period is full of references to the "delightful flaying," as he called it, that he was undergoing at the hands of every sixpenny critic in the country. Not content to vilipend the poem his critics proceeded to vilify the man, and Taylor was in some fear that certain of these ill-natured articles might be brought to the notice of Mary Agnew, who at this time was much worse. "This is a proper punishment to me for having defiled the temple of divine Poetry. Depend upon it," he wrote to George H. Boker, "I shall never do the like again, and I shall not fail to woo her with prayers and penances till the fault be expiated, and she admits me once more into her priesthood." As with the Apothecary in "Romeo and Juliet" it was Bayard Taylor's poverty and not his will that consented to this vulgar trial, and the bitter sense of degradation that he felt was the truest testimony to his nobility of purpose, and the surest prophecy of his future success.

The month following this episode was an anxious one. There was no longer any hope of Mary

Agnew's recovery. On October 24th they were married. For two months the young wife lingered, quietly patient, " radiantly beautiful," but not with the beauty of earth; then, " with no foes to pardon and no sins to be forgiven," she died, and in her grave Bayard Taylor buried the first period of his literary life.

Until the close of 1850 he had undergone but slight change of character. His first visit to Europe, his busy editorial career in New York, the revelation to him of fierce human passions in California, had not materially affected his early piety and youthful aspirations. He had remained through all the child of enthusiasm and faith. The censurings and complainings of the friends at Kennett, who looked upon him as on one fallen from grace, were scarcely recognized by him as long as that one angel face shone for him in the old home, and with sweet affection and tender sympathy made the trim Quaker land a Paradise. Now that that face had vanished Kennett was a painful place to him. He felt, too, the dull pain which followed upon the long continued anxiety. A disinclination to work possessed him. He was nervous and restless, and worn in mind and body. He matured his plans, long held in abeyance, for a visit to the Orient. He revised his poems, collected for publication the best

that he had written since the date of " Rhymes
of Travel" (1849), and so rolled a stone across
the irrecoverable and unforgettable past. He
looked into his financial affairs, found himself
three thousand dollars to the good, and the
owner of three shares of " Tribune " stock on
the first day of January, 1851, and of two more
on January 21st.

That he was closing one of the chapters of his
life not even his profound depression could prevent him from feeling. On New Year's Day,
1851, he wrote to George H. Boker, " This,
the beginning of the year, the turning-point of
the century, seems to me like the beginning of
a new career." And to James T. Fields he
wrote (April 19, 1851), " I am getting into a
very different sphere of thought, and feel that,
whether it be better or worse, I never can
wholly return to the themes I have hitherto
tried."

He sailed from Philadelphia, August 28, 1851,
on the City of Manchester, bound for Liverpool. All home affairs had been set in order,
Greeley had promptly consented to his absence,
and the editing of a " Cyclopædia of Literature
and the Fine Arts," for Putnam, had provided
him with the means of travel. He left behind
him his old life, and, as the crown and culmination of it, a volume of poems, " A Book of Ro-

mances, Lyrics, and Songs," published by Ticknor, Reed & Fields, soon after his departure.

In London he met the Brownings and John Kenyon and Lady Stuart Wortley, and went by way of Heidelberg and Nürnberg to Trieste, and thence to Smyrna and Alexandria. For two years and four months he was away from home. His experiences were strange, and the barbaric East gave him gorgeous days and solemn nights. The first year of his journey found him in Egypt, Syria, Palestine, and Asia Minor. Upon the Nile he writes, "Every day opens with a *jubilate*, and closes with a thanksgiving. If such a balm and blessing as this life has been to me, thus far, can be felt twice in one's existence, there must be another Nile somewhere in the world." [1] A fortnight before reaching the turning point on the White Nile he wrote the "Nilotic Drinking Song: " —

> "You may water your bays, brother poets, with lays
>   That brighten the cup from the stream you dote on,
>   By the Schuylkill's side, or Cochituate's tide,
>   Or the crystal lymph of the mountain Croton:
>   (We may pledge from these
>   In our summer ease,
>   Nor even Anacreon's shade revile us —)
>   But I, from the flood
>   Of his own brown blood,
>   Will drink to the glory of ancient Nilus!"

[1] *A Journey to Central Africa*, p. 86.

He passed beyond the utmost bounds of civilization, and up the Nubian Nile into Ethiopia. After he had reached Khartoum he proceeded by the White Nile to the country of the Shillooks. At this time the strangest rumors found place in the newspapers at home, now to the effect that Taylor had gone to the source of the Nile, and now that he was exploring the Niger, or losing himself in the enormous wilderness of equatorial Africa. His letters in the " Tribune " were eagerly looked for, and every exaggerated report of his wanderings found ready credence. Taylor had become a popular figure, and he was unconsciously building up, thousands of miles from home, the very reputation that he was least ambitious to possess. The secret of his immense vogue as a lecturer was the universal curiosity that he had excited as a traveler. Browning's " Waring " expresses the feeling that most persons had for Taylor. As the traveler who had penetrated the romantic East, — Vishnu land, " where whole new thousands are," — he carried with him an atmosphere of strangeness and remoteness and mystery. Longfellow dwells upon it in his verses upon the death of Taylor : —

> " Traveler, in what realms afar,
> In what planet, in what star,
> In what vast aerial space
> Shines the light upon thy face ? "

The most popular pictures of Taylor represented him in Oriental garb. The first " Putnam's " had him in Arab burnoose and turban, and Hicks's painting of him in Eastern dress and with Persian pipe was instantly recognized by every one who had read (and who had not read ?) " The Lands of the Saracen."

Bayard Taylor was the ideal traveler, and he was most at home in the Orient. His belief that in him the Palm and Pine commingled has already been referred to. He invariably assumed the garb of the people among whom he happened to live, and seemed to don with the dress, the language and the habits of the race. " It needed not," says E. C. Stedman, " Hicks's picture of the bronzed traveler, in his turban and Asiatic costume, smoking, cross-legged, upon a roof-top of Damascus, to show us how much of a Syrian he then was. We saw it in those down-drooping eyelids which made his profile like Tennyson's ; in his aquiline nose, with the expressive tremor of the nostrils as he spoke ; in his thinly tufted chin, his close curling hair, his love of spices, music, coffee, colors, and perfumes ; his sensitiveness to outdoor influences, to the freshness of the morning, the bath, the elemental touch of air and water and the life-giving sun. It is to be found in the ' Poems of the Orient,' where we have these traits reflected in diverse lyrics that make a fascinating whole. In them he seemed to give full vent to his flood of song." In only one respect did these Arab features belie the wearer of them. The Abyssinian sun had so burnt that aquiline nose, which was always thin (so thin that of it in Piatti's bust of him Taylor declared that it was " the thinnest nose ever cast in plaster "), that the skin had cracked, and there grew upon his face a permanent look of disdain which repelled from him many who had not learned the real sweetness of his nature, and gave him at times a reputation for coldness and pride which his gentle and generous life in no wise deserved.

In a letter to James T. Fields, dated Constantinople, July 14, 1852, Taylor writes, "If you could see me now you would swear I was a disciple of the Prophet. I am become

> " ' Long and lank and brown
>   As is the ribbed sea-sand,'

but I pray you mislike me not for my complexion. I wear the tarboosh, smoke the Persian pipe, and drop cross-legged on the floor with the ease of any tailor whatever. When I went into my bankers' they addressed me in Turkish. The other day, at Brousa, my fellow-Mussulmen indignantly denounced me as damned, because I broke the fast of the Ramazan by taking a drink of water in the bazaar. I have gone into the holiest mosques in Asia Minor with perfect impunity. I determined to taste the Orient as it was, in reality, not as a mere outside looker-on, and so picked up the Arabic tongue, put on the wide trowsers, and adopted as many Eastern customs as was becoming to a good Christian."

In his diary, under the date of November 5th, he writes, " I have a southern soul, it seems, for I feel strongest and happiest when I am where the sun can blaze upon me ; " and again he adds, " I am a worshiper of the sun. I took off my hat to him, as I stood there, in a wilderness of white, crimson, and purple flowers, and let him blaze away in my face for a quarter of an hour. And as I walked home with my back to him, I often turned my face from side to side that I might feel his touch on my cheek."

The climate of Khartoum affected him unfavorably. " He who lives in Khartoum in the hot season," he said, " must either sweat or die." He therefore turned away from " the silent fiery world of tawny sand and ink black porphyry mountains in the heart of Nubia," and reached Cairo, April 1, 1852, and Smyrna, April 22d. On horseback he proceeded to Jerusalem, Damascus, Aleppo, and through Asia Minor to Constantinople, where he arrived July 12th. He then set out for home, going first to

Malta, and thence by a small sailing-boat to Catania in Sicily, where he witnessed, August 17–20, the festival of St. Agatha which occurs but once in a hundred years. As he rode forth in the diligence from Catania, he saw the flames and heard the thunders of the eruption of Mount Etna. By way of Leghorn, Florence, and Venice he entered Germany, called at Gotha upon Mr. Bufleb, the companion of his voyage upon the Nile, and was again in London October 11, 1852.

He renewed some old acquaintances, met Mazzini, Miss Mitford, George Peabody, Mary Howitt, and a few other celebrities, but in less than three weeks he was away again from the foggy, sticky, " bituminous metropolis." His maledictions upon English sun and autumn rains recall Landor's growl that " one might live comfortably in England if he were rich enough to possess a solar system of his own."

His course now was to the south. Through the sleepless Bay of Biscay he proceeded to Spain, and by the India mail steamer reached Bombay, December 27, 1852. His heavy luggage he sent by steamer to Calcutta, and, rid of all impedimenta, he went overland by cart to Indore, Agra, and Delhi. Brief as his time was, he made a hurried and rough journey to the highest point in the Himalayas which could be reached in the winter season, and in less than two months traveled twenty-two hundred miles in the interior. But no rapidity of travel could rob his eye of the beauty or deprive him of the significance of the scenery and the life. At Dehra he stayed with Mr. Keene, the deputy marshal, the H. G. K. of " Blackwood's." At Benares he was the guest of Fitzedward Hall, the professor of Sanskrit.

When he had reached Constantinople in July he had found a letter from the " Tribune " office awaiting him. It contained a proposition to him to accompany Commodore Perry's expedition to Japan, the "Tribune" to supply the funds and to obtain him a place on board of the flagship. This last proved more difficult than his " Tribune " associates had foreseen, and Taylor was finally instructed to proceed to Hong Kong, where he would meet Commodore Perry, who had said that he would be very " happy to see Mr. Taylor. " It was Taylor's haste to reach the Chinese port that was hurrying him so rapidly across country to Delhi and Calcutta. After touching at Singapore he arrived in Hong Kong March 16, 1853. Upon the invitation of Captain Buchanan he went on board the Susquehanna and sailed to Macao and Shanghai. An ineffectual attempt was made to reach Nankin, and the Susquehanna returned

to Shanghai, where Taylor presented himself
to Commodore Perry, who had arrived from
Hong Kong, and received from him after some
delay and diplomacy the post of master's mate.
The rules of the service prevented Taylor from
writing a line for publication.   He kept a careful journal which he delivered to the Navy Department, but which he was never permitted to
recover.   It was consulted by Francis Lister
Hawks in his " Narrative of the Expedition of
an American Squadron to the China Sea and
Japan " (1856).

After four months' service Commodore Perry
gave the master's mate permission to resign, and
Bayard Taylor, after a letter to George H. Boker
written from the grotto at Macao " where our
brother Camoëns wrote the ' Lusiad,' " went by
steamer to Canton and embarked on the Sea-
Serpent, a merchant ship bound for New York
round the Cape of Good Hope, and, after a long
tumble about the Cape, and a brief halt at St.
Helena, he arrived in fourteen weeks (December 20, 1853) at New York.   Macaulay when he
sailed for India took with him the seventy volumes of Voltaire for playful diversion by the
way ; Taylor in his ocean transit committed
more than a score of poems to paper, rewrote
the letters which had been lost at sea, and completed the literary record of two years of travel.

His books of travel in their time were highly esteemed, for they told of striking adventure and splendid courage and persistence, and they still find a ready sale, although the demand for that class of literature has greatly fallen off. Their chief merit is reportorial. Taylor's object was to give correct pictures of foreign life and scenery, and he wisely left antiquarian research and speculation to abler hands. His books are, as he said, " a series of cosmoramic views." To him " a live Arab " was more interesting than "a dead Pharaoh." He had no ambition to build a reputation upon his prose, but his style was always perspicuous, and at times vivid. He resisted the temptation to write flamboyant descriptions, and wrote simply and concisely. His word pictures of architecture and scenery retain their place in the hand-books of foreign travel to voice the inarticulate emotion of the tourist, and his account of a hasheesh debauch and of an Oriental bath, in " The Lands of the Saracen," justifies the criticism that has named him " the best American reporter of scenes and incidents."

His protracted travels broke up or interrupted his associations in America. He returned from distant journeys to find remarkable changes in social and literary life, old cliques disbanded, and former friendships dissolved. The reputation that he had as a traveler, and the curiosity that the people showed in him, excited the envy of some of his fellows in the press. Malicious falsehoods concerning him were invented and circulated. One epigrammatic fiction more ingenious than the rest was widely repeated. It has become one of the best known anecdotes of literary men. The bare mention of the name of Bayard Taylor is sufficient to recall the statement that Humboldt once said that of all men he had ever known Taylor had traveled the farthest and had seen the least. The story was witty, and it had an air of verisimilitude. It was such a thing as Humboldt might have said, for Taylor made no pretensions to scientific knowledge ; he did not assume to know scientifically the geology and the sociology of the countries he visited. The things over which the author of " Cosmos " would have paused in delighted surprise Taylor does not see or at least says nothing about. He sketches the gay, the *bizarre*, the exterior life of the countries that he visits. The story nevertheless was entirely without foundation and was invented by Park Benjamin, who, upon his death-bed, acknowledged having originated it.

Taylor always explained the spiteful story by saying that Park Benjamin had asked him for a set of his works, and Taylor, feeling that he could not afford to make the present, had by his refusal to comply with the request excited Benjamin's enmity and desire for revenge.

"By-Ways of Europe" was a book of travels published by Taylor in 1869. It was the eleventh volume of travel that he had written and published. He believed it to be probably his last, and he prefaced it with "a familiar letter to the reader," in which, with his finger upon the reader's buttonhole, he relates the circumstances that led to the series of personal and literary experiences which his ten previous volumes had contained. "As I have been specially styled, for so many years and little to my own satisfaction, 'a traveler' or 'a tourist,' and in either character have received praise and blame, equally founded on a misconception of the facts and hopes of my life, I claim the privilege, this once, to set the truth before those who may care to hear it." ("By-Ways," p. 7.) He proceeds to tell how he was driven to his first tramp trip (1844) by the strong necessity of providing for himself sources of education which, situated as he was, could not be reached at home. It was as an obedient servant of the Press that he had gone to California and Mexico in 1849. "When, two years later, a change of scene and of occupation became imperative, from the action of causes quite external to my own plans and hopes, my first thought naturally was to com-

plete my imperfect scheme of travel by a journey
to Egypt and the Orient. I was, moreover,
threatened with an affection of the throat, for
which the climate of Africa offered a sure rem-
edy." ("By-Ways," p. 10.)

He admits that this free rambling was "a
grateful release from the drudgery of the editorial room. After three years of clipping and
pasting, and the daily arrangement of a chaos
of ephemeral shreds, in an atmosphere which
soon exhausts the vigor of the blood, the change
to the freedom of Oriental life . . . was like
that from night to day. With restored health,
the life of the body became a delight in itself;
a kindly fortune seemed to attend my steps; I
learned something of the patience and fatalistic
content of the races among whom I was thrown,
and troubled myself no longer with an anxious
concern for the future."

During a winter and summer trip to the far
North (1856–57), and a journey to Greece and
Russia which immediately followed, he found,
as he says, that his former enjoyment of new
scenes and the zest of getting knowledge at first
hand were sensibly diminished by regret for the
lack of those severe preparatory studies which
would have enabled him to see and learn so
much more. He was once lamenting his lack
of special knowledge when Humboldt said to

him, " But you paint the world as we explorers of science cannot. Do not undervalue what you have done. It is a real service ; and the unscientific traveler who knows the use of his eyes observes for us always without being aware of it." Dr. Barth and Dr. Petermann voluntarily confessed their interest in the power with which Taylor brought vividly home to thousands of firesides clear pictures of the remotest regions of the earth. The Duke of Argyll told Taylor that he was the cause of Tennyson's visit to Norway ; after reading " Northern Travel " Tennyson was determined to see the Northern lands.

At one time when the influence of Humboldt was upon him, the idea hovered before his mind of constructing " a *human* cosmos, which should represent the race in its grand divisions, its relation to soil and climate, its varieties of mental and moral development, and its social, political and spiritual phenomena, with the complex causes from which they spring." He read, in the East, Rückert's " Morgenländische Sagen und Geschichten," and Goethe's " West-Oestlicher Divan." He aspired after " the unshackled range of all experience." And while he did not hesitate to confess that to be styled " a great American traveler " had always touched him with a sense of humiliation, as if one should say " a great American pupil," he realized that he had gained in breadth of view and richness of life, and in " l'Envoi " to the " Poems of the Orient " he wrote : —

> " For not to any race or any clime
>   Is the completed sphere of life revealed ;
> He who would make his own that round sublime
>   Must pitch his tent on many a distant field."

CHAPTER III.

LECTURER AND LANDOWNER.

1854–1860.

BAYARD TAYLOR found a copy of "Eldorado" in a library at the foot of the Himalayas. He had been told by James T. Fields that his books were selling to travelers in England at every railway station. Despite these evidences of popular and unusual interest he was unprepared for the universal curiosity concerning him that he found upon his return to America. The "Tribune" letters had been widely and eagerly read, — "the 'Tribune' comes next to the Bible all through the West," Bayard wrote to his mother, — the adventures of his youth and the sad romance of his early manhood had fascinated the public, and there were many thousands from Maine to Wisconsin who were impatient to see the returned "Waring" — Avatar of Vishnu land.

In the early "fifties" the lyceum lecture system was at its height. In the West, particularly, popular education was supposed to be forwarded by lectures on every conceivable subject delivered in every imaginable manner. The prices paid to lecturers, in the Eastern States at least, were not magnificent. James T. Fields said humorously that he and Dr. Holmes were wont to get five dollars for a lecture, and that upon one occasion the lyceum refused to pay, because, said the chairman, " It wa'n't as good as we expected." George William Curtis tried the lecture platform to retrieve his fortunes from business calamity, and when he received fifty dollars for one evening he exclaimed jubilantly " I am now getting the price of a *prima donna.*" Still the fancy for lectures was sufficiently fresh and strong to insure to a popular past-master in the art an income more substantial than he could hope to earn with his pen.

Bayard Taylor was an excellent lecturer. His manner was easy, fluent, conversational. He told his story simply and frankly, and the story was one of absorbing interest. He wrote three lectures, — " The Arabs," " India," " Japan and Loo Choo," — that were vivid word-pictures of the lands and people they described. G. P. R. James once said that Bayard Taylor was the best landscape painter in words that he had ever known. And this art, the reporter's art, Taylor exercised without any attempt at " fine writ-

ing ; " he simply saw clearly the thing he described, and told what he saw in a plain way.

"I have a quiet laugh to myself now and
then," he said to J. T. Fields, "at the idea of
being a popular lecturer, I who have no faculty
for anything like oratory. I see how it is that
people are interested in what I say ; but that
does n't lessen the absurdity of the thing. I
care no more for the applause I receive from
lecturing than if it were bestowed on somebody
else ; the only advantage I am conscious of is,
that I can stand up in the face of the multitude
without feeling embarrassed."

Between January and May, 1854, he filled
ninety lecture engagements, even small towns
paying him fifty dollars a lecture, and in the
fall he delivered one hundred and thirty more.
In Baltimore he addressed an audience of four
thousand persons. A special train was run from
Canandaigua to Penn Yan, when he was lecturing at the latter place. "Vagabondage," Taylor
called the nomadic life he was now living, and it
quickly grew repugnant to him. "I am stared
at and pointed at," he wrote to his mother, "as
if I were the great Gyaskutos [*sic*] itself." To
R. H. Stoddard he wrote, "I have lectured nine
times since I saw you, and have had great success everywhere. Crammed houses, women carried out fainting, young ladies stretching their

necks on all sides and crying in breathless whispers, 'there he is! *that's* him!'"

Grace Greenwood tells of an interesting afternoon in the Old Corner Bookstore in Boston, when Taylor, in a weary and a somewhat petulant mood, dissuaded her from lecturing, saying that it was an occupation full of misery, that he himself detested it, and that an audience seemed to him no other thing than a collection of cabbage-heads. A few minutes later Mr. Emerson congratulated her upon the thought of lecturing, saying that there was recompense for all the hardships of the work in the kind words and the smiling faces and the bright eyes of the audience.

In this busy year (1854) he published in one season three books, "A Journey to Central Africa, or Life and Landscapes from Egypt to the Negro Kingdoms of the White Nile," [1] "The Lands of the Saracen, or Pictures of Palestine, Asia Minor, Sicily, and Spain," [2] and "Poems of the Orient." [3]

Even his buoyant spirits and abundant health drooped and flagged at times, not from stress of work so much as because of the tedious journeys, the ill-cooked food, and the tiresome con-

[1] Published August, 1854.
[2] Published October, 1854.
[3] Published October 27, 1854.

gratulations the thousandth time repeated. His lecture engagements often carried him into a zone of tough steaks, bad water, and no beer, whose miseries he was constrained to endure until his deliverance into a mellower region. " I am quite fagged out," he writes to his mother, " not with speaking, but with traveling, and with being shown up, introduced, questioned, visited, and made to visit, handshaken, autographed, honorary membershiped, complimented, censured, quizzed, talked about before my face by people who don't know me, written about in the papers, displayed on handbills, sold on tickets, applied to for charitable purposes, and the Lord knows what else." Where his audiences were intelligent and sympathetic Taylor found the work pleasant enough. Pittsburgh he preferred to all other cities to lecture in. Prosperity came with the popularity. However distasteful the work he was doing, it brought ever nearer that independence of fortune which was to make possible his scheme of life. The " Tribune " was paying comfortable dividends, his books of travel were selling rapidly, seven thousand copies of the " Journey to Central Africa," and a like number of " The Lands of the Saracen," having been ordered before publication. He was preparing for a Western house a " Cyclopædia of Travel," for which, though perfunctory task work, he was to receive five thousand dollars.

He had cause to congratulate himself and to rejoice, to believe the singing birds musicians, the flowers fair ladies, and his steps no more than a delightful measure or a dance.

Before his return from Europe in 1853, the Pusey farm, a tract of eighty acres near Kennett, which he had long wanted to possess, was purchased for him. In 1855 he added to it about forty-five acres which he bought from his father, and forty acres, with an ancient stone farmhouse, obtained from his uncle. It was his purpose to build a large house which should be the home of all his family. He improved the land, planted evergreen trees, and while busy in remote parts of the country lecturing was never far in thought from Kennett, and constantly sent money to his mother for the purchase of trees and shrubs.

Two brief vacations he allowed himself in 1855. He took his father and mother in May to the Mammoth Cave, which, he says, is beyond " Vathek's Hall of Eblis ; " and in August, as representative of the " Tribune," he accompanied Lieutenant Maury and Professor Silliman and a scientific party to put down the submarine telegraph between Nova Scotia and Newfoundland. Soon after his return from the latter trip he

published in September "A Visit to India,
China and Japan in the year 1853," and followed it about the middle of November with
"Poems of Home and Travel," and a revised
edition of "Views Afoot" with a new preface.

The winter of 1855–56 was unusually severe.
Again Taylor had undertaken a heavy burden
of lecture engagements. In February, 1856, he
broke down in Boston and upon medical advice
canceled all his engagements, abandoned his ir-
regular life, returned to New York and cleared
away all arrears of work, and completed every
literary obligation. Never before did he do so
much in the same space of time. Between the
first of April and the seventeenth of June, he
finished nine hundred royal octavo pages of the
" Cyclopædia of Modern Travel," " besides preparing thirteen maps and a variety of cuts and
looking after the printing, engraving, etc."

Another period of his life closed when, with
all tasks well ended, he sailed for Europe, on
July 9th, taking with him his two sisters and
his youngest brother. For four months he
played the complete part of guide, philosopher
and friend. He traveled familiar ground, seeing
afresh the famous places through the delighted
eyes of his companions. In Germany he was
surprised and more than pleased at the way in
which he was received. He wrote to his mo-

ther, to whom very frankly he related circumstances which it would have savored of vanity or affectation to disclose to another, "Dresden is the literary city of Germany, and I met with all the authors living there. I was delighted to find that they all knew me. When I called on the poet Julius Hammer, he was at his desk, translating my poem of 'Steyermark.' Gutzkow the dramatist, Auerbach the novelist, Dr. Andrée the geographer, and others whose names are known all over Europe, welcomed me as a friend and brother author. We had a grand dinner together the day before I left. The Dresden papers spoke of me as a distinguished guest, and published translations of my poems. In fact I think I am almost as well known in Germany as in the United States."

He settled his sisters and brother at a pension in Lausanne while he returned for a second and longer visit to Gotha, from whence he started by way of Coburg, Dresden, and Berlin to carry out his old intention of a journey to the land of the midnight sun. With his companion, Braisted, a sailor, who was acting as his valet, he set forth from Stockholm, December 15, 1856, and in two months made the tour of Lapland.

He traveled "nearly twenty-two hundred miles, two hundred and fifty of them by reindeer, and nearly five hundred within the Arctic

circle." Reindeer travel he compares to a frisky
sturgeon harnessed to a "dug-out" in a rough
sea. The book that records his journey is
"Northern Travel: Summer and Winter Pictures of Sweden, Denmark and Lapland"
(1857). It is a book of the thermometer. Taylor's satisfaction at his endurance of extreme
cold seems to take precedence of his interest in
the life of the country. At Kautokeino he saw
a day without a sun. "The snowy hills to the
north, it is true, were tinged with a flood of
rosy flame, and the very next day would probably bring down the tide mark of sunshine to
the tops of the houses. One day, however, was
enough to satisfy me. You, my heroic friend,[1]
may paint with true pencil and still truer pen
the dreary solemnity of the long Arctic night:
but, greatly as I enjoy your incomparable pictures, much as I honor your courage and your
endurance, you shall never teach me to share
in the experience. The South is a cup which
one may drink to inebriation; but one taste
from the icy goblet of the North is enough to
allay curiosity and quench all further desire."
("Northern Travel," p. 132.)

As he left the solitude of the North, he writes:
"Not the table-land of Pamir in Thibet, the
cradle of the Oxus and the Indus, but this lower

[1] Dr. Elisha Kent Kane.

Lapland terrace, is entitled to the designation of the ' Roof of the World.' We were on the summit, creeping along her mountain rafters, and looking southward, off her shelving eaves, to catch a glimpse of the light playing on her majestic front. Here for once we seemed to look down on the horizon, and I thought of Europe and the tropics as lying below. Our journey northward had been an ascent, but now the world's steep sloped downward before us into sunshine and warmer air." (" Northern Travel," p. 147.)

He returned to Gotha in May, 1857, and spent some time in excursions into the forests and mountains. He accompanied his sisters and his brother to Bremen, and then visited England. Thackeray, whom he had met in 1855, introduced him to Tennyson, with whom he spent two days.

T. Buchanan Read took him to Hammersmith to call on Leigh Hunt, then seventy-three years old. Hunt showed him his curious collection of locks of hair of the poets. " That thin tuft of brown silky fibres," writes Taylor describing his visit, " could it really have been shorn from Milton's head? I asked myself. ' Touch it,' said Leigh Hunt, ' and then you will have touched Milton's self.' ' There is a love in hair, though it be dead,' said I, as I did so, repeating a line from Hunt's own sonnet on this lock."

To complete his northern travel, Taylor sailed from Hull (July 3) for Christiania, and traveled to Drontheim. He saw the midnight sun at the North Cape, "and had quite enough of the North." A journey through Dalecarlia to Stockholm, and to Copenhagen where he met Hans Christian Andersen and Professor Rafn, completed his quest after new sensation.

And now occurred the happiest event of his life. His companion, six years before, when traveling upon the Nile, was a German landowner whose acquaintance he had made *en route* from Smyrna to Alexandria. Between Mr. August Bufleb, the German, and Bayard Taylor there immediately grew up the most affectionate friendship. Each showed for the other unbounded devotion and generosity. How romantic and how real the attachment was may be gathered from Bayard Taylor's letter to his mother (December 19, 1851) : " For two days before our parting he could scarcely eat or sleep, and when the time drew near he was so pale and agitated that I almost feared to leave him. I have rarely been so moved as when I saw a strong, proud man exhibit such an attachment for me. He told me he could scarcely account for it, but he felt almost ready to give up all his engagements to return home and accompany me. I told him all my history, and showed him the

portrait I have with me.[1]   He went out of the
cabin after looking at it, and when he returned
I saw that he had been weeping."

When Taylor returned from Newfoundland,
in September, 1855, he received a letter from
Mr. Bufleb presenting him with a beautiful bit
of property in Gotha.   "Whilst you," writes
Bufleb, "were dedicating your glorious work on
Central Africa to me, I was setting in order for
you the most cherished part of my possessions."
Taylor and his companions reached Gotha the
following August, and made their home in this
charming place which the thoughtful affection
of Mr. Bufleb had provided.   "The house,"
writes Taylor, "is furnished in antique style
with high-backed, red velvet chairs, Brussels
rugs, sofas, mirrors, flower-stands, matches and
cigars on the table, tea, sugar, etc., in the cup-
board, and beer in the cellar.   Nothing was forgotten ;   the smallest things were all in their
places, and here I live like a prince."   Here, too,
he became acquainted with the gentle lady,
Marie Hansen, niece of Mrs. Bufleb and daughter of Peter Andreas Hansen, the eminent as-
tronomer and director of the Ducal Observatory,
to whom he was married in Gotha October 27,
1857.   Through the remaining twenty-one years
of his life she was his loyal helper in all his toil,

[1] His picture of Mary Agnew.

and after his death she collected with affectionate care his large correspondence that was dis-
persed through many hands, and with Horace
E. Scudder edited the admirable and complete
" Life and Letters of Bayard Taylor."

After his marriage, Taylor went with his wife
to London, where he superintended the publication of " Northern Travel," which was issued
simultaneously in New York by G. P. Putnam,
and in London by Sampson, Low & Co.

The farthest point reached by Taylor upon
his first visit to Europe, it will be remembered,
was Rome.   Circumstances constrained him to
give up " the thrilling hope," as he called it,
"of climbing Parnassus and drinking from
Castaly."   The long deferred visit to Greece he
was now about to make.   He left Gotha in December (1857) and, a voyager on the Ionian
blast, hailed the bright clime of battle and
of song.   He touched at Corfu, the ancient
Corcyra, saw the smoke leap up from Ithaca as
the returning Odysseus saw it, and recalled at
Leucadia his own verses upon " The Death of
Sappho," now blended with Byron's " Leucadia's far-projecting rock of woe."   Their vessel
anchored off Missolonghi, where Byron's stormy
life ceased, and at Patras Taylor's feet first
pressed the " haunted holy ground."   On Christmas Day his eye swept the Bay of Salamis, and

the same day he walked up the street of Hermes and in the street of Æolus engaged apartments for the winter in the Hotel d'Orient.

Bayard Taylor knew no more Greek than John Keats, but he had appropriated with kindred intuition the spirit of Greek life and art. Every moment ran itself for him in golden sands. Delicious indeed was the first breakfast in Athens, with honey from Mt. Hymettus. The lovely isles of Greece took his reason prisoner. Excursions were made to Crete, to the Morea, and to Thessaly; and through Mycenæ and Tiryns he rode with unknown treasures under his feet. He began the study of modern Greek and learned sufficient to answer the necessities of travel. Ancient Greek he did not take up until the last years of his life. William D. Howells, in "Harper's Magazine" for May, 1894, writes, "I remember that I met him once in a Cambridge street with a book in his hand which he let me take in mine. It was a Greek author, and he said he was just beginning to read the language at fifty; a patriarchal age to me of the early thirties! I suppose I intimated the surprise that I felt at his taking it up so late in the day, for he said, with charming seriousness, 'Oh, but you know, I expect to use it in the other world.' Yes, that made it worth while, I consented; but was he sure of the other world?

' As sure as I am of this,' he said; and I have always kept the impression of the young faith which spoke in his voice, and was more than his words."

Alfieri in his delightful Autobiography tells how he began Greek at forty-eight, " reading the aspirates, accents, and diphthongs as they are written and not as they are stupidly pronounced by the modern Greeks, who have an alphabet of five *iotas*, making their language a continual *iotacism*, more worthy of the neighing of horses than the most harmonious tongue in the world." Taylor, who never forgot anything, found his Romaic serviceable, when, in long railroad journeys, he refreshed himself by studying ancient Greek, and he therefore used the modern pronunciation and read his Homer, as Alfieri would have said, with " vile *iotacism*."

A journey was made into Crete, of which Taylor records nothing memorable. In a monastery among the ruins of Aptera, where he spent a night, he found " the sacerdotal fleas were as voracious as Capuchin friars."

He reached Corinth at the time of the great earthquake of February 21, 1858, and went south into Sparta, where he was entertained by relatives of Dr. Kalopothakes, who for more than thirty years has taken American visitors to Greece under his hospitable care.

At the Piræus Taylor saw Mrs. Black, "the Maid of Athens" to whom Byron sang in impossible and ungrammatical Greek. Mavrocordatos, old and blind, the friend and ally of Byron, was still living. Dr. Schöll, in whose arms Otfried Müller died, and who was one of the physicians who attended upon Byron at Missolonghi, recounted the closing scene of the poet's life to Taylor, while Mr. Finlay, the historian of Mediæval Greece, told him the circumstances under which Byron contracted his fatal illness.

From Athens (May 6th) Taylor departed to Constantinople, where he said he noticed but three changes since 1852: that Pera is lighted with gas, that the hotels have raised their prices five francs a day, and that the dogs of Stamboul no longer bark at Giaours. He returned by the Danube to Gotha, where Mrs. Taylor was established in her former home, and again set out on the third of June for Poland and Russia, returning to Gotha at the end of July. His only child, Lilian, was born August 3, 1858.

Before the first of October, the time fixed by Taylor to return to America, occurred the three hundredth anniversary of the University of Jena, of which he has left a vivid account in "At Home and Abroad." Here at the Kneipe he made the interesting acquaintance of Fritz Reuter, and tells with delight of his volleys of Low German fun.

On the 24th of October the Taylors arrived at Kennett Square.

Deep in his heart Bayard Taylor bore a warm affection for Chester County, the place of his birth. His love of country life and the ambition to furnish a generous roof-tree for his family seemed now about to be gratified; in the repose of his own home, and in the peace of a quiet neighborhood, he could develop the poems that were kindling in him and which he believed the world would not willingly let die. Upon the spot which he had chosen for his ideal and idyllic home the ground was now broken, and while the work went forward Taylor established his family with Richard H. Stoddard and his family in Brooklyn, and then departed upon another lecturing tour in which the entire winter was consumed. When summer came the building of the house engaged his attention. At this time he was writing sketches of travel for the " New York Mercury." He had purchased the stereotype plates of his works from Mr. Putnam after the latter's business embarrassments, and Putnam now acted for him, as for Washington Irving, in the capacity of agent. To his books of travel Taylor added, in 1859, " Travels in Greece and Russia, with an Excursion to Crete," and " At Home and Abroad : A Sketch Book of Life, Scenery and Men."

From California, whither he had gone on a three months' lecturing tour, he returned delighted and surprised at the magic growth of the country. He wrote of it: —

ON LEAVING CALIFORNIA.

O fair young land, the youngest, fairest far
  Of which our world can boast, —
Whose guardian planet, Evening's silver star,
  Illumes thy golden coast, —

The marble, sleeping in thy mountains now,
  Shall live in sculptures rare;
Thy native oak shall crown the sage's brow
  Thy bay, the poet's hair.

Thy tawny hills shall bleed their purple wine,
  Thy valleys yield their oil;
And Music, with her eloquence divine,
  Persuade thy sons to toil.

Till Hesper, as he trims his silver beam,
  No happier land shall see,
And earth shall find her old Arcadian dream
  Restored again in thee!

He was more than ever weary of lecturing, — two hundred and seventy lectures he had given in eighteen months. His eagerness to occupy the great house that was now approaching completion, and his excitement at the nearness of that period when time and peace should be his to walk in the fields of his heart and to dedicate the best of himself to poetic endeavor, increased

his irritation at the uncongenial tasks that
pressed upon him. He went with his family
to the old homestead until May, 1860, when
they moved into the new home which he called
" Cedarcroft," and with him he took his father
and mother and his two sisters. The house had
cost him seventeen thousand dollars, and the
stereotype plates of his books had cost him five
thousand more. All debts were paid and he
seemed about to enter into the enjoyment of
a rest that he had well earned. He invited
the " Return of the Goddess : " —

> " Not as in youth with steps outspeeding morn,
>   And cheeks all bright, from rapture of the way,
> But in strange mood, half cheerful, half forlorn,
>   She comes to me to-day.
>
> " Does she forget the trysts we used to keep,
>   When dead leaves rustled on autumnal ground,
> Or the lone garret, whence she banished sleep
>   With threats of silver sound ?
>
> " Does she forget how shone the happy eyes
>   When they beheld her, how the eager tongue
> Plied its swift oar through wave-like harmonies,
>   To reach her where she sung ?
>
> " How at her sacred feet I cast me down ?
>   How she upraised me to her bosom fair,
> And from her garland shred the first light crown
>   That ever pressed my hair ?
>
> " Though dust is on the leaves, her breath will bring
>   Their freshness back : why lingers she so long ?

The pulseless air is waiting for her wing,
  Dumb with unuttered song.

"If tender doubt delay her on the road
  Oh let her haste to find the doubt belied!
If shame for love unworthily bestowed,
  That shame shall melt in pride.

"If she but smile, the crystal calm shall break
  In music, sweeter than it ever gave,
As when a breeze breathes o'er some sleeping lake,
  And laughs in every wave.

"The ripples of awakened song shall die
  Kissing her feet, and woo her not in vain
Until, as once, upon her breast I lie —
  Pardoned, and loved again!"

"When I build a house," Taylor had said in his youth, "I shall build it upon the ridge, with a high steeple from the top of which I can see far and wide." Cedarcroft is conspicuous by its lofty tower and stands upon high ground about a mile north of the built-up portion of Kennett Square. On the eastern side of the Kennett road, within a stone's throw of the domain of Cedarcroft, at the end of a long lane of tall old cedars, is a two-story gray house, with a wooden porch and rustic dooryard which was the home of Taylor's childhood. Over the front arch of the main entrance to Cedarcroft is a square of white stone bearing the legend

BAYARD MARIE TAYLOR.

1859.

In the rear of the house is a belt of cedars and behind these rise gigantic forest trees. Not even the mighty oaks of Charlecote Park, where young Shakespeare went poaching, Taylor was fond of saying, equal these secular trees of Cedarcroft. There is but one open space in the zone of trees, where the sloping sward ends to the southeast, at a distance of a quarter of a mile, in an artificial pond. Doubtless it was when this violet-starred bank flashed upon the inner eye which is the bliss of solitude that Taylor wrote : —

> "The violet loves a sunny bank,
> The cowslip loves the lea ;
> The scarlet creeper loves the elm,
> But I love — thee."

No one can ever quite know what manner of man Bayard Taylor was who has not known him as host and friend at "Towered Cedarcroft." All the future circumstances of his life were indissolubly knit to this rural home. With what affection he watched its rise, with what joy he witnessed its completion, can only be appreciated when we enter into Taylor's ardent nature and realize how he panted for recognition and for sympathy and how dear to him was the

native soil of his loved Chester County. Out of
that soil and from his own domain he dug the
clay and baked the bricks to build these massive
walls. His was the primal eldest passion, the
love of the earth! Like Scott at Abbotsford he
desired a large estate, rich acres that he might
call his, and a mansion, baronial in its extent,
not for shallow pride and ostentation, but that it
might be the comfortable home of his kindred
and furnish free-hearted hospitality to his friends.
And like Scott at Abbotsford, and Burke at
Beaconsfield, the home that he had longed for
and toiled for became a burden and a weary
weight, prematurely ending his overtaxed life.

The great entrance door opened upon a broad
hall and wide oaken stairway, to the left of which,
and facing south and west, was the splendid
library room. Here Taylor carried forward his
literary work. Here he wrote " The Poet's
Journal," " The Picture of St. John," and " Home
Pastorals ; " two of his novels, " Joseph and his
Friend," and " The Story of Kennett," besides
his translation of " Faust," and vast quantities
of miscellaneous task-work. Here while he hurried the busy pen he smoked his narghile, or
his cigar ; and here he entertained his friends,
— poets, journalists, painters — to whom the hall
doors swung widely open.

Busts of Shakespeare, Goethe, Bryant, and

Virgil overtopped the bookcases, and framed autographs of Thackeray and Tennyson hung upon the walls. The great house with its broad acres was a splendid monument to the unflagging zeal of its humbly proud master, who but fifteen years before had gone forth a poor lad to see the world, and to win the recognition that now in such heaping measure was already his.

Taylor's rambles in England had impressed him with the importance of adorning the physical aspect of America by reproducing within it the sweetness and beauty of the domestic and religious spirit of the older civilization. The welfare of the future, he taught, lies in the worship of beauty. He knew that American life needed nothing so much as *repose*. Donald Grant Mitchell, "the Horatian classic of American letters" as William Winter has so happily called him, who always had a strong fondness for rural life, in 1869 edited the "Hearth and Home," for which Taylor wrote articles upon landscape gardening. In Mitchell's home at Edgewood Taylor drew plans for the projected house at Cedarcroft, and in conversation with Mitchell agreed that while the old halls and manor houses of England are the best models for such a structure, yet our brighter sky and southern summer require a lighter and more cheerful aspect. He once wrote to Mitchell,

"No man can do better work for this country and people than to create such a taste
for country life as will elevate and refine the
character of our country society." He enjoyed
greatly the cultivation of his acres. A new
addition to his garden he hailed with a delight
scarcely less keen than that with which he
greeted the idea of a new poem. The seed of a
melon from the Caspian bought at Nijni-Novgorod, mixed with "Mountain Sweet" and
planted in Cedarcroft garden, produced a new
and capital variety of watermelon. Seed of
the Latakia (Laodicea) tobacco brought from
Egypt was planted in the same rich soil, and
soon the "great vegetable" was thriving at
Cedarcroft.

Miss Laura Redden (Howard Glyndon)
when staying at Cedarcroft asked Bayard Taylor why he had created a pond at the foot of
the lawn. Taylor replied that it was useful as
well as ornamental as he intended to drown in
it all his disagreeable neighbors. And indeed
those neighbors were not few. He had been
but a short time at Cedarcroft before he found
himself estranged from his old associates. The
neighborhood had two passionate interests, Abolition and Temperance. Across the county
from Kennett to Longwood Meeting were various stations of the Underground Railway.

W. L. Garrison, Oliver Johnson, Wendell Phillips, Starr King, Lucretia Mott and all the notable abolitionists had traveled the Kennett roads and had spoken at yearly meeting at Longwood. There Anna Dickinson had held aloft her white arm and cried that she would be glad and proud if colored blood coursed in her veins. The restraint and outward calm of the sober Quaker community when stirred by such sentiments of humanity burst into lightning-like passion.

The fancy of total abstinence had become with them a vital principle. Without it there was no salvation. Taylor had acquired in his travels and in his experience in cities a rational conception of life. He had learned that in exercise and not in repression was life's chief benefit and virtue.

His "Alongshore" letters to the "Tribune" in 1875 contained a sensible defense of nutritious and wholesome ale over limestone water and hayseed tea. He was a fit and faithful student of Aristology, which Mortimer Collins says is the art of having the best dinner in the best way. He was wont to describe what he chose to call "the cooking belt" in America, which continues south from West Chester, New York, through Chester County, Pennsylvania, to the terrapin and canvas-back of the

Maryland market. A profuse dinner at the northern end of the belt Cooper has described in " The Spy," when the procession of waiters at the Locusts bring on " whole flocks of pigeons, certain bevies of quails, shoals of flat-fish, bass, and sundry woodcock ; " and the produce of the Chester and Lancaster farms have given a traditional and enviable reputation to the West Chester dinners in Pennsylvania.

The people of Kennett were offended by the manner of Bayard Taylor's life. The wine upon his table, the beer and whiskey consigned to him from Philadelphia and New York and taken through the town to Cedarcroft were cause of grave concern to his friends and acquaintances. They remonstrated with him ; and he resented the remonstrance. The open, honest life he lived was interpreted by them as hostility and defiance. A physician of Kennett censured him for his manner of life. Taylor retaliated by introducing him into the novel of " Hannah Thurston " as an impertinent temperance crank. He could have no sympathy or patience with the narrow intolerance and impertinence that would compel others to live the life of the community.

They, with intemperance of speech, assailed his temperance of life, and malicious falsehoods were engendered and circulated, and found their unclean ways into journals, and led to petty annoyance and to ignominious contests. Cynical skeptics who wailed the loss of a stomach or the incapacity of a palate, and anæmic ascetics who diluted their anacreontics with water and celebrated with timid voices the sparkle of Apollinaris, found a virtue in denouncing Bayard Taylor's "indulgence." The same people found Longfellow guilty of a serious misdemeanor when he declared that the best thing he had found in England was Bass's ale. The whole truth is that Taylor was a robust man of vigorous appetite. He ate heartily, drank sufficiently, and worked enormously.

"Earth-Life" was written by him out of sheer weariness of the perpetual prate that he heard about him of "soul-life" and "spirit's mission." The voice of his irritation escapes again in "In My Vineyard."

> "The secret soul of sun and dew
>   Not vainly she distilleth,
> And from these globes of pink and blue
>   A harmless cup she filleth:
> Who loveth her may take delight
>   In what for him she dresses,
> Nor find in cheerful appetite
>   The portal to excesses.
>
> "Yes, ever since the race began
>   To press the vineyard's juices,
> It was the brute within the man
>   Defiled their nobler uses;
> But they who take from order joy,
>   And make denial duty,

Provoke the brute they should destroy
By Freedom and by Beauty ! "

He wrote to his old friend, J. B. Phillips,
" There are no such quietly impertinent and
meddlesome old Betties in domestic matters as
some old male Quakers." He withdrew himself
more and more from the people whose simple
lives had seemed so beautiful when seen from
the thronged pavements of New York. In his
correspondence there is a frequent note of
discontent and disillusionment: " I live in a
loneliness which is rarely pleasantly broken "
(October 31, 1870), and " Pennsylvania is vastly
behind Massachusetts, but that is partly owing
to the stagnation of Quakerism. All the appreciation I get comes from New England. Pennsylvania gives me nothing but sneers and abuse,
and I am a little tired of it."

While this unfortunate sentiment existed in
Kennett, Taylor was not without his loyal
friends. When he occasionally drove, farmer-
like, into West Chester in a dilapidated old
wagon with a leisurely horse, and smoking a
cigar of the period, tolerable in a high wind,
there were many faces that brightened with
pleasure and many hands that were extended
in hearty greeting. One literary friendship de-
serves more particular attention, as it lent much
pleasure to Taylor's life, and profited him

greatly in his most ambitious work. Twenty miles away in an adjacent county, in the beautiful region of Wallingford, was the summer home of Dr. Horace Howard Furness. When Bayard Taylor was engaged upon his translation of "Faust," and was puzzling over difficult tangles that other translators had found "too intrinse t' unloose," he was wont to clear his mind by a visit to Lindenshade, as the estate at Wallingford was called, and a talk with Dr. William H. Furness, for whose German scholarship and poet's intuition Taylor had the highest respect and veneration. The days at Lindenshade were golden ones in Taylor's calendar. Almost the only literary atmosphere he breathed was at the Furness' home. Dr. H. H. Furness was beginning those studies in Shakespeare which were to culminate in the "New Variorum edition," the most magnificent monument that ever has been reared to the memory and the knowledge of Shakespeare. His sister, Mrs. Wister, was engaged upon those translations of German novels that have been more popular than any other books rendered from German into English.

After a happy summer's day spent in talk upon the second part of "Faust," Taylor addressed the following poem (which is now for the first time printed) to his friends.

GRUSS AN LINDENSCHATTEN.

Der glückliche Tag ist vorüber,
  So lange ersehnt und gehofft:
Wir gestehen, es wäre uns lieber
  Wenn solche genössen wir oft.

Gespräche im Schatten der Linden,
  Gesang und den perlenden Wein:
Wo Freuden wie diese wir finden,
  Fliesst ruhig das Leben, und rein.

Gemüth harmonirt mit Gemüthe;
  Gedanken entfalten sich frei:
Ja, das ist die einzige Blüthe
  Die duftet wenn Sommer vorbei!

So lasst uns die Stimmung bewahren,
  Und gönnt uns das heitere Glück,
In diesem und kommenden Jahren
  Zu rufen die Tage zurück!

Die Linden die summen noch immer
  Von Stimmen und Liedern und Spiel;
Über Alles verweilt noch ein Schimmer,
  Es waren der Freuden so viel!

Doch wir, ach! wir sitzen so einsam,
  Und öd' ist das grüne Gefild:
Geniesst man die Stunden gemeinsam,
  Da giebt 's ein vollkommenes Bild!

Es sehnen sich nun uns're Bäume
  Nach den Gästen, die fehlen so lang
Die Säle, die häusliche Räume,
  Sie lauschen auf Lust und Gesang.

So kommt, eh' verwelket die Matten !
Dass der Tag uns bald wieder erschein',
Wo uns Cedern, nicht Linden, beschatten
Im fröhlichen, lieben Verein ! [1]

To this Dr. W. H. Furness replied :—

" MY DEAR BAYARD TAYLOR, — I trust you
do not mean to claim these lovely German verses
(I know no measure more delicious — one can
afford to let the rhymes take care of themselves,
come or stay away as they please — bless me !
what a long parenthesis this is, — but hold on)
as original, because if you do one of the enclosed
papers will prove them to have been translated
from the English. I grant your translation im-
proves upon the original, but still it is too literal
to be anything but a translation. You thought it
would not be found out, but I read your verses
over only once or twice and instantly the original came to me, but I don't know whose it is, or
where it is to be found." (July 25, 1869.)

With this playful charge of plagiarism Dr.
Furness sent the following beautiful translation
of Taylor's German verses.

CEDARCROFT TO LINDENSHADE.

The day that we longed for is over,
    It is numbered with days that are gone,
How blest would this life be, if often
    Such calm pleasant days would return.

[1] The poem is in the style of Kotzebue : —
    " Wir sitzen so fröhlich beisamen."

We sat and we talked 'neath the lindens,
  We had poems and pearly bright wine, —
How smoothly life passes and purely
  When with it such joys we entwine.

Attuned was each heart to the others,
  Our thoughts and our fancies flowed free.
Ah! these are the blooms that are fragrant
  When summer has long ceased to be.

Then let us, their fragrance preserving, —
  The seasons are flying so fast, —
In this and in all coming summers
  Call back the bright days that are past.

Still, still do they whisper, those Lindens,
  Of voices and music and play,
Over all there still lingers a shimmer,
  So full was the joy of that day.

But we, ah! we sit now so lonely,
  And bare are the green fields around.
Only when we are merry together,
  Only then does enjoyment abound.

These old trees of ours now long for
  The guests whom they so long have missed;
The dear household places, — the parlor
  Awaits for the song and the jest.

So come, let the day be repeated,
  Ere the glories of summer shall fade,
Where not Lindens but evergreen Cedars
  Shall cover us all with their shade.

Taylor never shut himself up to write. His
library doors were always open, for the presence

of his guests or of the members of the household did not disturb him in his work. And those guests were numerous. Often he cast aside the pen to greet a chance caller, or to welcome in a friend of fame in art or letters. His generous hospitality was freely given to every visitor ; he was the best conditioned and unwearied spirit in doing courtesies. When Cedarcroft was finished in the summer of 1860, Taylor gave a housewarming, and he and Richard Henry Stoddard wrote a play, as Stoddard said, " for the delectation of the good, honest country folk, who had no idea that they witnessed what the world's people would call a theatrical performance." The bill of the performance, set up with flaming head-lines, read : —

CEDARCROFT THEATRE !

GREAT ATTRACTION !

Saturday, August 18, 1860,

will be presented for the first time a

NEW COMEDY

In One Act, — entitled

LOVE AT A HOTEL !

By the World-Renowned Dramatic Authors,

MR. B. T. CEDARCROFT

and

MR. R. H. S. CUSTOMHOUSE.

"The 'comedy' was a great success," said Stoddard, "and deserved to be (before a country audience), for there was not an original scene, situation, thought, or word in it." [1]

Whittier and Lowell had visited Taylor at the old farm at Kennett. Emerson, Curtis, Boker, Stedman, Aldrich, Greeley, and many artists and authors came to Cedarcroft. When E. C. Stedman was Taylor's guest in June, 1865, a picnic on the Brandywine was planned. The feast was rudely disturbed by the advance of a herd of cattle, one hundred strong, who deployed in line of battle, and threatened the security of the small company. "Mr. Stedman, in great glee, flung himself upon the back of a fine short-horned steer, and Bayard Taylor, like a sacrificial priest, took hold of one of the horns, and, swinging his staff, led the astonished animal and his rider about in triumphal procession." [2]

Taylor has celebrated this incident in his sonnet to E. C. S., Christmas, 1865 : —

"When days were long, and o'er that farm of mine,
   Green Cedarcroft, the summer breezes blew,
   And from the walnut shadows I and you,
Dear Edmund, saw the red lawn-roses shine,
Or followed our idyllic Brandywine
   Through meadows flecked with many a flowery hue,
   To where with wild Arcadian pomp I drew
Your Bacchic march among the startled kine,

[1] *The Atlantic Monthly*, February, 1879.
[2] *Life and Letters*, p. 432.

You gave me, linked with old Mæonides,
 Your loving sonnet, — record dear and true
 Of days as dear: and now, when suns are brief,
And Christmas snows are on the naked trees,
 I give you this — a withered winter leaf,
 Yet with your blossom from one root it grew."

NOTE. — Fire damaged a part of Cedarcroft in Christmas week, 1894. An addition that had been built to the house was destroyed, and the woodwork of the library was scorched and burnt.

CHAPTER IV.

NOVEL WRITING.

1861–1866.

IT is a commonplace to speak of Bohemianism in New York about 1860. Yet to speak accurately, there were no Bohemians in New York. There was much convivial and unconventional life, there were those who were careless what they did to spite the *bourgeois* world, but there was no real Bohemianism. The poets and journalists, though depending on small and precarious incomes, had washerwomen and lodgings, and generally paid their debts, notwithstanding that at times they were detained by their landlady for indifference to rent-day, and sometimes locked up in Jefferson Market for pranks that are now popularly believed to be performed by college sub-freshmen only. To appreciate what Bayard Taylor did, it is necessary to understand the background of his life in New York, and to know the sort of thing that was going on. The conditions of authorship had greatly changed from what they were

when he first came to the city. The Knickerbocker school had faded out. A brilliant circle
of young writers of erratic lustre and small
reverence had appeared. Washington Irving,
"the first literary ambassador from the New
World to the Old," died in 1859; and in the
same year death claimed in this country Rufus
Choate and William Hickling Prescott, and in
England Leigh Hunt, Thomas De Quincey and
Lord Macaulay. In that year " The Knickerbocker Magazine," the tower of literary strength
in New York, came to an end; and N. P.
Willis published his last book, " The Convales-
cent." The cessation of " The Knickerbocker "
and of " Putnam's Magazine " marked the passing of the old régime.

In 1857 the " Atlantic Monthly " was begun
in Boston. Holmes named it ("not because
it was a notion"), Lowell became its editor-
in-chief, and all the well-known writers of the
country were among its contributors. " The
Saturday Press " was started in New York, October 23, 1858, by Henry Clapp, Jr., a cynical
journalist who could throw more bitterness into
a single sentence than any man of his period.
Thomas Bailey Aldrich was associate editor,
and Fitz-James O'Brien was dramatic editor.
In December, 1860, the publication was discon-
tinued, but after some years it was resumed

with the appropriate explanation: " This paper was suspended for lack of funds ; it is now recommenced *for the same reason.*" John Brougham had begun " The Lantern," an illustrated comic paper, in 1852. " Mrs. Grundy," commenced by A. L. Carrol and edited by Charles Dawson Shanly, and " Vanity Fair," edited by Frank Wood, followed the " Saturday Press." Among the contributors to these vivacious and reckless journals were E. G. P. Wilkins, W. L. Symonds, Henry Neill, N. G. Shepherd, C. D. Shanly, C. I. Gardette, Fitz-Hugh Ludlow, C. F. Browne (Artemus Ward), George Arnold, Fitz-James O'Brien, E. C. Stedman, T. B. Aldrich, and William Winter.

In New England, upon the " Atlantic Monthly," there was culture and tradition, order and decorum. Among the contributors to the New York papers there was fever and recklessness, gayety and melancholy. No respect was shown by the younger writers for "the various camphorated figure-heads which were then an incubus upon American letters."

John Brougham gave weekly dinners at Windust's, near the original Park Theatre, which were attended by the Aladdins who " trimmed the wick of the ' Lantern.' " The staff of " Vanity Fair " met on Fridays in the old editorial rooms, 113 Nassau Street, and drank, and smoked, and discussed the next issue. The general gathering place of the clan, however, was in Pfaff's beer cellar in Broadway. If the New England authors, serene upon their transcendental heights, taught the virtues of plain living and high thinking, the frequenters of Pfaff's believed as potently in high thinking and hard drinking. George Arnold, the laureate of the long table in this dingy cellar, is authority for it that

" We were all very merry at Pfaff's."

Hither came Walt Whitman, whose cause the " Saturday Press " had taken up with its accustomed vigor, looking like the Phidian Jove. Here too came O'Brien, disfigured by pugilism, a gypsy of letters whose long periods of idleness were broken by such sudden raptures of creation as " A Fallen Star " and " The Diamond Lens ; " " Fitz - Gammon O'Bouncer " William North styled him. Here came " Ned " Wilkins, feeding on Montaigne, as George Arnold fed upon Balzac ; and the cynical Clapp, who originated the saying, " A self-made man, yes, and worships his creator ; " and Shepherd, who wrote the " Roll Call," and Shanly, who should be remembered for his " Rifleman, shoot me a fancy shot."

Mr. William D. Howells has recently related the impression made upon him by a visit to Pfaff's in 1860 — " At one moment of the orgy, which went but slowly for an orgy, we were joined by some belated Bohemians whom the others made a great clamor over; I was given to understand they were just recovered from a fearful debauch; their locks were still damp from the wet towels used to restore them, and their eyes were very frenzied. I was presented to these types, who neither said nor did anything worthy of their awful appearance, but dropped into seats at the table, and ate of the supper with an appetite that seemed poor. I stayed, hoping vainly for worse things till eleven o'clock, and then I rose and took my leave of a literary condition that had distinctly disappointed me."

Taylor, as a companion of Willis, who was styled by " Vanity Fair " the " pink of the press," was not of the " Bohemian " crew, although he was an occasional visitor at Pfaff's. The " Albion " had published a truculent article upon him, and " Vanity Fair " launched at him mild squibs. Although Taylor held himself aloof from the noisy midnight life, he had many valued friends in the " snapping turtle press," and he was in no small degree influenced by the life that was about him. Without doubt he was saved from the experience that so many

of the young journalists of the great city knew,
by his foreign travel and his touch upon European culture and Oriental calm.

Stoddard, Taylor and O'Brien were frequently
amiable rivals in the rapid making of burlesque
rhymes. Stoddard in his reminiscences thus recalls these nights of literary frolic. "We sat
around a table and whenever the whim seized
us, which was often enough, we each wrote down
themes on little pieces of paper, and putting
them into a hat or box we drew out one at ran-
dom, and then scribbled away for dear life. We
put no restriction upon ourselves: we could be
grave or gay, or idiotic even ; but we must be
rapid, for half the fun was in noting who first
sang out, 'Finished.' It was a neck and neck
race between Bayard Taylor and Fitz-James
O'Brien, who divided the honors pretty equally,
and whose verses, I am compelled to admit, were
generally better than my own. Bayard Taylor
was very dexterous in seizing the salient points of
the poets we girded at, and was as happy as a
child when his burlesques were successful. He
reminded me, I once told him, of Katerfelto

> " 'With his hair on end
> At his own wonders.'

He blushed, laughed, and admitted that his clev-
erness pleased him, and he was glad that it

pleased us also. ' It is good sport,' he remarked ;
' but poetry, — that is very different.' "

A permanent friendship, too, was formed with
William Winter, for whose complete mastery of
the eighteenth century manner Bayard Taylor
had the highest respect and admiration. In
1876, when Taylor was occupied with the Centennial Ode, he was requested to prepare a poem
for the Society of the Army of the Potomac.
Unable to discharge both tasks he transferred
the latter to Winter, who read at the Academy
of Music in Philadelphia, June 6, 1876, his com-
memorative poem, " The Voice of the Silence."

A small circle of writers still eddied about
Willis and Morris and the " Home Journal ; "
the " Bohemians " foregathered at Pfaff's, and
the " respectables," the oldest and strongest men
in art and letters, belonged to the Century Associ-
ation which, in 1846, had grown out of the Sketch
Club and the Column Club. Washington Irving
named the " Century," and S. F. B. Morse,
W. J. Hoppin, A. B. Durand, William Cullen
Bryant, Henry T. Tuckerman, G. C. Verplanck,
Gouverneur Kemble and John F. Kensett were
members. Bayard Taylor was made a centurion
in 1851. Another semi-literary organization
was the Press Club, which originated in 1852
while Kossuth was in America ; Henry Ward
Beecher was its secretary, and Charles A. Dana,

Henry J. Raymond, John Bigelow and Parke
Godwin were among its members. The club
dined at stated occasions at the Astor House,
and Bayard Taylor was occasionally of the party.

From first to last Taylor's relations were clos-
est with the " Tribune " set. He was one of the
earliest stockholders of the paper and served it
in one capacity or another from his first entrance
into New York until his death. Horace Greeley,
a few weeks before January 1, 1849, invited
certain persons employed in leading positions in
the several departments of the paper to join him
as co-partners. Bayard Taylor and Charles A.
Dana were among those who availed themselves
of this opportunity. Among Taylor's associates on the Tribune were Sydney Howard Gay,
Charles T. Congdon, Edward H. House, and
William H. Fry (who came from Philadelphia).
Taylor had reverential cordiality for George Ripley and was intimate with Charles A. Dana,
George William Curtis and James S. Pike. He
knew A. D. Richardson and George W. Smalley,
but not well. He had high regard for the literary judgment of Col. John Hay, and the varied
experiences of both had given them abundant
interests in common.

Such was the literary and social life of New
York when Bayard Taylor was scurrying across
the continent on a lecturing tour or peacefully

cultivating his strawberries, figs and pomegranates at Cedarcroft.

Meanwhile a portentous shadow was falling across the country. The terrible urgency of civil war, and an immense physical activity, were temporarily to retire art, and to direct genius to more immediate and practical ends. The best years of the young writers of the " Saturday Press " and the other Bohemian publications of New York were absorbed and consumed in the wild years of the Rebellion. When the war was over, a certain phase of literary history had passed forever from America. At the outbreak of the struggle there was an instant stagnation in literature. Publishers were fearful, authors were enlisting. Repose is essential to permanent beauty. Great works ripen slowly. The awful pageantry of civil strife for those who felt the sharpness of the quarrel had no romantic glamour.

During 1860 Bayard Taylor had published a revised and enlarged edition of the " Cyclopædia of Modern Travel," and continued his letters of travel to the " Tribune." He contributed to the " Mercury " various papers upon California, and translated the article upon Martin Luther from Gustav Freytag's " Pictures of Life in Germany during the last Four Hundred Years." His German friends, the Buflebs, visited Cedarcroft, and with them Taylor made a trip to the White Mountains and up the Saguenay.

As the Presidential election of 1860 drew near the political excitement ran high. At a mass meeting of Republicans held upon the old battle-field of the Brandywine, Bayard Taylor presided and said : —

"It is a national, not a party struggle in which we are engaged ; for the question whether our national policy shall or shall not be based upon the recognition of the natural rights of man — upon the rights of labor, the untrammeled freedom of thought and speech — upon those principles, in fact, on which the progress of the race depends — concerns not merely a party, but all mankind."

In the middle of October Taylor resumed lecturing, and soon had reason to know the intense party feeling that existed in the country. We were then in what Harriet Martineau called "our martyr age," when eloquence was dirt cheap, and the eloquent speakers often suffered seriously for their advocacy of unpopular principles. A mob arose against George William Curtis in Philadelphia as against Garrison in Boston. A storm of popular indignation burst in Brooklyn upon Bayard Taylor for his defense of the course taken by Curtis. Girt about by policemen Taylor delivered his lecture in Philadelphia the following week. A lecture bureau in the South canceled its engagements with him after this open definition of his position, and a wordy war followed in which Taylor had distinctly the best of the argument. With the actual burst of war he sold a share of "Tribune" stock to enable his youngest brother, Frederick, to enlist in the army; this he said was his contribution toward putting down the Rebellion. In the spring of 1861 he abandoned his New York home and moved all his possessions to Cedarcroft. In May he sailed with his wife for Germany, and proceeded to Gotha, whence he made an excursion into the Franconian mountains. Numerous descriptive letters were sent to the "Tribune" and to the "Independent." He returned to New York in August and went at once to Cedarcroft, where he wrote a number of magazine articles, notably one upon Hebel, "the German Burns," and a story, "The Haunted Shanty." His lecture upon "The American People in their Social and Political Aspects" was prepared at this time. The year closed with another lecturing tour in the northeast which was neither extensive nor profitable, for, as Taylor wrote, "These war times are hard on authors; the sword of Mars chops in two the strings of Apollo's lyre!"

Early in March, 1862, Taylor was in Washing-

ton as war correspondent of the "Tribune," and
before the end of the month it was proposed
that he should accompany Simon Cameron, the
newly appointed minister to Russia, as Secretary
of the Legation. Here was an opportunity to
accomplish under Russian protection that exploration of Central Asia which he had so long
wished to make. The salary, too, was sufficient
to relieve him from the hated drudgery of lecturing. He was assured that Cameron would
return in the fall, leaving him acting *chargé
d'affaires*, and that it was quite probable that
the ministry itself would ultimately be his. He
sailed on the Persia in May, 1862, with Mr.
Cameron's party. For a time Bayard Taylor
and his family were the guests in Paris of James
Lorimer Graham, a fellow-member of the Century Club. They then went on to Gotha,
whence Taylor continued with Simon Cameron
to St. Petersburg.

During the remainder of the year much writing was done : a Quaker story, " Friend Eli's
Daughter," a simple tale of Philadelphia and
the valley of the Neshaminy, and several sketches
of travel were sent to the " Atlantic Monthly ; "
a poem on the one thousandth anniversary of the
Russian Empire pleased Prince Gortschakoff,
by whom it was shown to the Emperor, who sent
word to Bayard Taylor that he was touched and

delighted. Two excursions taken in July and at the close of August furnished material for "Atlantic" papers. The first was "A Cruise on Lake Ladoga;" Taylor was the first American who had visited the northern portion of the lake. The other, the account of which was published in 1864 under the title "Between Europe and Asia," was to the Nijni-Novgorod fair, where he witnessed a remarkable performance of Macbeth by Ira Aldridge, the Baltimore mulatto who was called the "African Roscius," and who was a pupil of Edmund Kean. "A mulatto Macbeth in a Russian theatre with a Persian and Tartar audience!" To the Tartar camp on the hill of Novgorod, Taylor went for an experimental draught of *koumiss*, the fermented milk of mares. "Having drunk palm-wine in India, *samshoo* in China, *saki* in Japan, *pulque* in Mexico, *bouza* in Egypt, mead in Scandinavia, ale in England, *bock-bier* in Germany, *mastic* in Greece, *calabogus* in Newfoundland, and — soda-water in the United States, I desired to complete the bibulous cosmos in which *koumiss* was still lacking." ("By-Ways of Europe," p. 79.) The taste, Taylor declared, was that of "aged buttermilk mixed with ammonia." The subject of a curious Russian story, "Beauty and the Beast," that was published in 1865, was also at this time obtained.

Simon Cameron left Russia in September, and Taylor continued as *chargé d'affaires* until May 7, 1863, when Cassius M. Clay, the new minister, was received by the Emperor. One month after the responsibility of the Russian Legation had been fastened upon Bayard Taylor he sent a dispatch to the Department of State, which is quoted here as illustrating the character of his diplomatic correspondence, and also the regard in which he was held at the Russian court : —

MR. TAYLOR TO MR. SEWARD.

LEGATION OF THE UNITED STATES,
ST. PETERSBURG, *October* 29, 1862.

SIR, — I have the honor to report to you that, immediately after the receipt of your dispatch No. 14, of September 26, I applied for an interview with Prince Gortchacow, for the purpose of delivering into his hands the letter of his excellency the President to his Imperial Majesty Alexander II. My request was at once granted, and an early hour the next day was appointed ; but the Prince having in the mean time been summoned to the town of Gatschina, some thirty miles from here, to confer with the Emperor, the interview was postponed until to-day.

After having received the President's letter, which he promised to present to his Imperial

Majesty without delay, the Prince entered upon a conversation concerning American affairs, which I deem so important that I hasten to report it, while his expressions are yet fresh in my mind, and can be communicated to you with the greatest possible exactness.

He began by stating in the strongest terms his concern at the course which events are taking in the United States. "Your situation," said he, "is getting worse and worse. The chances of preserving the Union are growing more and more desperate. Can nothing be done to stop this dreadful war? Can you find no basis of arrangement before your strength is so exhausted that you must lose, for many years to come, your position in the world?" I answered that the critical period in the fortunes of the war seemed now to be passed; our arms were again victorious, and, could the military strength of the rebellion be once fairly broken, it would be almost impossible for it to maintain itself longer. "It is not that alone," said he, "but the fury that seems to possess both sides, — the growth of enmities which are making the gulf continually wider between the two sections. The hope of their reunion is growing less and less, and I wish you to impress upon your government that the separation, which I fear must come, will be considered by Russia as one of the greatest possible misfortunes."

" To loyal Americans," I answered, " separation seems nothing less than national ruin, and, precisely for this reason, there can be no negotiations at present with the rebel authorities. They would listen to no terms which did not include separation, and hence the War is still a terrible necessity. I have hopes, however, that a change may occur before the term of grace allowed by the President's proclamation expires. Have you noticed that the State of North Carolina is already taking some action on the subject?" " Yes," said he, " I have seen it. . . . Russia alone has stood by you from the first, and will continue to stand by you. We are very, very anxious that some means shall be adopted, — that any course should be pursued which will prevent the division that now seems inevitable. One separation will be followed by another; you will break into fragments. . . . You know the sentiments of Russia," the Prince exclaimed with great earnestness. " We desire above all things the maintenance of the American Union, as one indivisible nation. We cannot take any part more than we have done. We have no hostility to the Southern people. Russia has declared her position and will maintain it. There will be no proposals for intervention. We believe that intervention could do no good at present. Proposals will be made to Russia to join in some plan of interference. She will refuse any invitation of the kind. Russia will occupy the same ground as at the beginning of the struggle. You may rely upon it, she will not change. But we entreat you to settle the difficulty. I cannot express to you how profound an anxiety we feel, — how serious are our fears."

We were standing face to face during the conversation, and the earnest, impassioned manner of the Prince impressed me with the fact that he was speaking from his heart. At the close of the interview he seized my hand, gave it a strong pressure, and exclaimed, " God bless you ! "

Although disappointed in his ambition for the ministry Taylor was glad of the insight he had had into diplomatic affairs. It was in no small measure due to him that Russia continued friendly to the Union when the Southern Confederacy appeared to be victorious, and a proposition was submitted by France to England and Russia that the three powers should conjunctively propose " to the belligerent parties in America to agree to an armistice of six months." Taylor submitted to Prince Gortchakoff, with whom his relations were more than friendly — even confidential — a detailed statement of the

national debt of the United States; "the estimated annual revenue under the new laws; the
additions made to the active force of our armies
during the last three months; the number of
iron-clad vessels in process of construction and
the important movements already commenced
in the West and on the seacoast." The statement of facts which he had drawn with great
care and presented with clearness and force was
intended to convince Gortchakoff that an armistice at this time could only be of advantage to
the rebellious states, and that no proposition
of the kind could be entertained by the federal government. President Lincoln expressed
through William H. Seward his gratification at
Bayard Taylor's performance, even though the
action was a departure from the strict line of
duty of the *chargé d'affaires.* The communica-
tion had dispelled the despondency and allayed
the impatience of the imperial government of
Russia, and it elicited from Gortchakoff the assurance " that the policy of Russia in regard
to the United States is fixed, and will not be
changed by the course adopted by any other
nation."

After Bayard Taylor had acquainted Minister
Clay with the business of the legation, and written to the President that he would not remain
under any conditions, he went to Gotha, where

he awaited dispatches which he was assured that he would receive from Washington. Mr. Cameron wrote that the government felt that Taylor had been treated rather shabbily, when for party reasons the office of minister had been given to another, and that it was altogether likely that amends would be made by sending him on a special mission to Persia, to cement more firmly the friendly alliance with Russia, whose ambition to advance upon the frontier of Persia was well understood. While awaiting dispatches, Taylor made a ten days' trip to the Bohemian forest, was entertained by the Duke of Saxe-Coburg Gotha at Castle Kallenberg, near Coburg, and paid his last visit to Rückert. June 30th he left Gotha for a four weeks' tour of Switzerland and the Italian lakes. Upon his return he received the news of his brother's death in the battle of Gettysburg, and he immediately returned home, sailing August 29th on the Scotia. No explanation was forthcoming of the tedious delay in forwarding the dispatches from Washington. President Lincoln, surprised at his return, said that he had believed him to be in Persia. Secretary Seward alone knew why instructions and funds had not been sent to him two months before in St. Petersburg.

What Taylor thought of Seward's duplicity

and intrigue he expressed in the sonnet entitled
" A Statesman."

> " He knew the mask of principle to wear,
>   And power accept while seeming to decline ;
>   So cunningly he wrought, with tools so fine,
> Setting his courses with so frank an air,
> (Yet most secure when seeming most to dare,)
>   He did deceive us all : with mien benign
>   His malice smiled, his cowardice the sign
> Of courage took, his selfishness grew fair,
> So deftly could his foiled ambition show
>   As modest acquiescence.   Now, 't is clear
>   What man he is, — how false his high report ;
> Mean to the friend, caressing to the foe ;
>   Plotting the mischief which he feigns to fear :
>   Chief Eunuch, were but ours the Sultan's court ! "

Pilloried by Taylor's personal anger and patriotic indignation, in companion sonnets, stand
Secretary Seward and President Johnson.   To
the latter the lines to " A President " are addressed.

> " Thou, whom the slave-lords with contemptuous feet
>   Spurned in their double insult — taunting thee,
>   As born of Labor and of Poverty,
> With scorn in thine abasement most unmeet
> How dost thou find their false embraces sweet !
>   How so insanely blind, thou canst not see
>   What shameless scoffs in their applauses be ?
> So took the drunken slave, in Roman street,
> The homage of his master's mocking mirth :
>   And thou, who might'st have lifted up thy race,
> Dost rather take from Toil its dignity,
>   And unto ignorance addest fresh disgrace.
> But we shall sweep that system from the earth
> Which gave us Treason, war, and lastly — thee ! "

A restless intellect caused Bayard Taylor to try his hand at all forms of literature. It was also with the hope of working a lucrative literary vein that would take the place of the repugnant lecturing trade, that he undertook the composition of a novel. The work was begun in 1861, and before he left the country to assume the duties of the legation at St. Petersburg he had written seven chapters. It was finished in Russia and published November, 1863, in New York and London under the title "Hannah Thurston, A Story of American Life."

The novel was dedicated to George P. Putnam. Tennyson once said that he never knew an honest publisher until he became acquainted with Macmillan. It is well known that Campbell defined a publisher as the author's natural enemy. Taylor's friendship for Putnam and for Fields was an interesting example of the understanding and sympathy that are popularly supposed not to exist between publisher and author. The encouragement of Mr. Putnam at a critical moment of Taylor's young and timid life had cheered him in the long toilsome career he was to run.

The scene of the story is said to be central New York. The events occur in the village of Ptolemy on Atauga Lake, upon the northern side of the watershed between the Susquehanna and the rivers which flow into Lake Ontario. Despite the distinctness of topographical definition, and the near neighborhood of Ptolemy to Anacreon, Tiberius, Nero Corners and other names whose classical origin and antique lexical relish bespeak the nomenclatorial fancy of Simeon De Witt, — who, out of Lempriere's Dictionary, gave to commonplace New York villages the glory that was Greece and the grandeur that was Rome, — no one familiar with Pennsylvania and its people could for a moment fail to recognize in the happenings of the story and the dialect of its characters the life of Chester County.

Mr. Maxwell Woodbury, the hero, has returned from wandering over the world and intends to resume his life in the home of his childhood. The delight with which he greets the old scenes, familiar to him after twenty years, and the generosity with which he seeks to create " a warm atmosphere around his future home," are soon chilled by the petty slanders that the village breathes, and the tyranny of shallow and mistaken lives. Immediately before the publication of " Hannah Thurston," Taylor had gone through an unpleasant literary experience from which he was still smarting. The publishers of his poem, " A Poet's Journal," into which he had introduced certain moods of his mind and life, advertised the work as the record of his own experience. It was humiliating to Taylor even to seem to have unlocked his heart to public gaze, and the distress that the unhappy announcement occasioned him was real and lasting. In the preface to " Hannah Thurston " he protested against the popular superstition that an author must necessarily represent himself in one form or another, saying, " I am neither Mr. Woodbury, Mr. Waldo, nor Seth Wattles." One cannot avoid, however, reading into the book some of Bayard Taylor's experience at Cedarcroft. When he says of Maxwell Woodbury : " In the dreams of home which haunted him in lonely hours, on the banks of the Hoogly or the breezy heights of Darjeeling, Lakeside always first arose, and repeated itself most frequently and distinctly," it is of his own dreams, when lotos-eating in Egypt, or tanking in Syria, that he is thinking. He too, like Woodbury, had been first excited, then wearied by the atmosphere of the city after " he had slowly and comfortably matured his manhood in the immemorial repose of Asia." And like Woodbury " he simply wished to have a home of his own — an ark of refuge to which he could at any time return — a sheltered spot where some portion of his life might strike root."

" Hannah Thurston " might be called a prose

parallel of Tennyson's "Princess." It is the merest thread of a story, and almost without a plot. The characters are types, not individuals. The heroine is a good and interesting personality ; the hero is but a quintain, a mere lifeless block. The book is a very obvious satire of the fads and "isms" of the hour. All the characters are possessed by the most curious crotchets, — spiritualism, vegetarianism, teetotalism and abolition come in for their share of honest and wholesome rebuke. The Reverend Mr. Styles fears that so many lights at the sewing union "looks a little like levity ; " Mrs. Waldo, the reasonable wife of a reasoning clergyman, " was the oleaginous solvent, in which the hard yelk of the Mission Fund, the vinegar of the Cimmerians, and the mustard of the Abolitionists lost their repellent qualities and blended into a smooth social compound." In the society of Ptolemy " Scandal was sugar-coated in order to hide its true character : love put on a bitter and prickly outside, to avoid the observation of others ; all the innocent disguises of society were in as full operation as in the ripened atmosphere of great cities."

The villain of the story is the spiritualistic medium, Mr. Dyce, who, at a séance, is trapped by Mr. Woodbury's servant, who smears soot upon the piano keys ; and when light is admitted to the chamber the soot is upon the very material hands that in the darkness had played the weird music that thrilled the hearers with its spiritual origin and import. Woodbury, recalling with repugnance the occurrences of the evening, says to himself : " Better a home for the soul within the volcanic rings of yonder barren moon with no more than the privacy it may command in this life, than to be placed on the fairest star of the universe, and be held at the beck and call of every mean mind that dares to juggle with sanctities."

The great sewing union at Ptolemy, the spiritualistic séance, the meeting in favor of " Women's Rights," and the " temperance " camp-meeting, are all definite and innocent and more or less vulgar phases of American life as Bayard Taylor saw it ; and that which he saw he reported with his usual downright perspicacity of speech. At the entrance to the grove where the Annual Temperance Convention was to be held, " venders of refreshments had erected their stands, and displayed to the thronging visitors a tempting variety of indigestible substances. There was weak lemonade, in tin buckets, with huge lumps of ice glittering defiantly at the sun ; scores of wired bottles, filled with a sarsaparilla mixture, which popped out in a rush of brown suds ; ice-cream, the cream being eggs beaten

up with water, and flavored with lemon sirup;
piles of dark, leathery ginger-cakes, and rows of
glass jars full of candy-sticks; while the more
enterprising dealers exhibited pies cut into
squares, hard-boiled eggs, and even what they
called coffee. . . . After an appropriate prayer
by the Rev. Lemuel Styles, a temperance song
was sung by a large chorus of the younger
members. It was a parody on Hoffman's charming anacreontic, 'Sparkling and Bright,' the
words of which were singularly transformed.
Instead of —

> "'As the bubbles that swim on the beaker's brim
>   And break on the lips at meeting,'

the refrain terminated with

> "'There's nothing so good for the youthful blood
>   Or so sweet as the sparkling water!' —

in the style of a medicinal prescription. Poor
Hoffman! Noble heart and fine mind, untimely
darkened! He was at least spared this desecra-
tion; or perhaps, with the gay humor with which
even that darkness is still cheered, he would
have parodied the parody to death." It was at
this memorable convention that Mr. Grindle, in
a burst of marvelous rhetoric, referred to "the
hookah filled with its intoxicating draught," and
to the tottering steps of those into whose brains
"the fumes of sherbet have mounted."

Hannah Thurston, like Tennyson's Princess, whose surrender to love she reads and understands when her own heart is touched and her cold reason yields, at last "lays her masculine ambition in the hands of love."

The book was widely read, and commented upon with favor by the judicious and with indignation by the "reformers." Taylor was charged with misrepresentation and exaggeration. He replied that far from being exaggerated, the picture of the community was subdued. Hawthorne wrote to him, "The book is an admirable one, new, true, and striking, — worthy of such a world-wide observer as yourself, and with a kind of thought in it which does not lie scattered about the world's highways." Even the London "Spectator" bowed its crested head to say that it was "half inclined to suspect that Bayard Taylor had placed himself in the front rank of novelists."

While Putnam was printing fifteen thousand copies of "Hannah Thurston" in the fall and winter of 1863, Taylor was continuing a long poem, translating German, delivering his new lecture on "Russia and her People," and soliciting in Canada an English copyright for his novel.

The success of this first attempt at fiction was instantaneous. It appeared in Germany in translation, in Russian at St. Petersburg, and in Swedish at Stockholm. Taylor was encouraged to try a second novel. In New York, March 14, 1864, he began "John Godfrey's Fortunes; Related by Himself. A Story of American Life," and the book was published by Putnam in November. The summer in which it was written was fully occupied with house affairs and farm duties, a brief lecturing tour, poetry and translation, and magazine articles. In October Ticknor & Fields printed "The Poems of Bayard Taylor" in the beautiful and popular "Blue and Gold" edition.

Taylor wrote with such rapidity that he could complete a duodecimo volume in a fortnight. His industry of hand was amazing. He seemed never to weary, and his handwriting was exceptionally neat and fine. A comparison of letters written in his seventeenth year and in his fiftieth shows almost no change of hand. His penmanship and his style were formed early and changed little. In the long manuscript of "Faust" there is scarcely a misformed or carelessly made letter. He was a genuine artist in black and white, and his highest happiness was to sit from morn till dewy eve, smoking a cigar that was not too good, and filling page after page with his neat chirography. A surprising instance is recorded of his facility and speed. In a night and a day he read Victor Hugo's voluminous "La Légende des Siècles," and wrote for the "Tribune" a review of it which fills eighteen pages of his "Essays and Literary Notes," and contains five considerable poems which are translations in the metre of the original.

"John Godfrey" was written amid all manner of interruptions and in "the languor of an African summer," between March 15th and August 11th. It contains five hundred and eleven pages, or five hundred and ninety-four pages of Taylor's closely written manuscript. The crudities of style and the infirmities of construction in "Hannah Thurston" and "John Godfrey" are to be ascribed to the tearing speed at which they were written; and necessity's sharp pinch was the promoter of that speed. It was not so with poetry. With the exception of an occasional impromptu like "Icarus," the hundred verses of which were dashed off without pause and without blot or erasure, Taylor would spend hours over a couplet, fashioning it to the figure in his mind. But prose was with him purely pedestrian. He built no reputation on it, and was content that it should supply him with the means to live and to write poetry. Poverty has doubtless done more than wealth in the literary world; but in that world, too, it is no mean happiness to be seated in the mean, and the prayer of Agur is the petition of wisdom. Taylor declared that he sang better after the thorn was pulled out of his breast : " Freedom from pecuniary anxiety," he said, " gives my brain a genial glow, a nimble ease, a procreative power, which I never feel at other times." Fitz-James Stephen, when he was appointed to a judgeship, wrote to Lord Lytton that he felt like a man who had got into a comfortable carriage on a turnpike road after scrambling over difficult mountain paths. In like manner Bayard Taylor, when the year 1865 closed with a comfortable surplus of income, drove his " new tandem " — prose by day and poetry by night — smoothly and well, and with a glad content.

While not an actual sketch of the author's life, " John Godfrey's Fortunes " is a reminiscence of certain moods of that life and of literary and social experiences in New York. It is no wonder that the readers of the book continued, maugre the author's protest, to see in it a personal history, when they read of John Godfrey's birthplace : " The Cross-Keys lay aside from any of the main highways of the county, and the farmers around were mostly descendants of the original settlers of the soil, a hundred and fifty years before. Their lives were still as simple and primitive as in the last century. Few of them ever traveled farther than to the Philadelphia market, at the beginning of winter, to dispose of their pigs and poultry. A mixture of the German element, dating from the first emigration, tended still further to conserve the habits and modes of thought of the community. My maternal grandfather Hatzfeld was of this stock, and many of his peculiarities, passing over my mother, have reappeared in me, to play their part in the shaping of my fortunes."

It was Taylor's habit to gather the traits and peculiarities of his characters from various sources. Not one is drawn entirely from life, but the reader who is familiar with Taylor's surroundings can see just where he has appropriated the old materials that he has so dexterously welded into new creations. There are memories of Fitz-James O'Brien in Mr. Brandagee; and at least one whimsy of Estelle Ann Lewis — Poe's "rival of Sappho" — is remembered in the account of "Adeliza Choate," who tells Godfrey: "I feel the approach of Inspiration in every nerve. . . . It always comes on about three o'clock in the afternoon when the wind blows from the south. I change my dress and put on a long white gown which I wear at no other time, take off my stays, and let my hair down my back." It was only with her hair streaming over her shoulders that the " female

Petrarch," the "rival of Sappho," was able to obey the Muse.

The short stories that Taylor contributed to the magazines, and some of which were reprinted in the volume, " Beauty and the Beast: and Tales of Home " (1872), were usually founded upon incidents in Chester County history or tradition.

The Quaker widow, in the ballad, recalling after fifty years — that seem " but one long day, one quiet Sabbath of the heart " — the little romance of her marriage, says : —

> " Indeed 't was not the least of shocks,
> For Benjamin was Hicksite, and father Orthodox."

In lives that seemed to have little more of change or excitement than the Vicar of Wakefield's migrations from the brown bed to the blue, and back again from the blue bed to the brown, Taylor found color and incident enough to weave an innocent romance. In the story of " The Strange Friend," a Quaker, Henry Donnelly by name, arrives from Adams County and rents a farm at Londongrove. He and his family " become a permanent part and parcel of the remote community, wearing its peaceful color and breathing its untroubled atmosphere." De Courcy, the son with " the outlandish name," rides a gallant horse, dresses a little more elegantly than his membership prescribes, and is frequently seen to ride up the Street Road " in the direction of Fagg's Manor, towards those valleys where the brick Presbyterian church displaces the whitewashed Quaker meeting-house." The tragical death of the lad is almost immediately followed by the arrival of a long-expected agent from Europe, who brings to the strange friend assurance that his long voluntary exile is over, that his estate is free, and that he can now return as Lord Henry Dunleigh to Dunleigh Castle.

Even here it was not fiction that Taylor was writing, but history. Henry Hamilton Cox, who had inherited a heavily encumbered landed estate in Ireland, came to Pennsylvania and lived in obscurity first in York County and then in Chester County, until the income arising from the estate had cleared it of debt. He lived as a member of the Society of Friends until 1817 when he returned to Ireland, throwing his broad-brimmed hat, it is said, into the ocean. He was the author of " The Pennsylvania Georgics."

Caleb Taylor and Ellwood Garrett, natives of Chester County, on May 29, 1851, were at Castle Rock, overlooking the rocks where the notorious highwayman Fitzpatrick — the terror of the county, who scoured the country at his will between the Schuylkill and the Susquehanna — is supposed to have secreted his plunder. Mr. Garrett spoke of writing a story about Fitzpatrick, but he afterwards suggested the theme to Bayard Taylor, who converted the robber into the Sandy Flash of his third and best novel, " The Story of Kennett " (1866). It is a true idyl of Pennsylvanian country life, and there are in it sharply defined characters and vivid flashes of tragedy. It has made the name of the little town of Kennett familiar in literature : " The lovely pastoral landscapes which I know by heart have been copied, field for field and tree for tree, and these you will immediately recognize," he writes in his Prologue addressed to his friends and neighbors of Kennett. " Many of you will have no difficulty in detecting the originals of Sandy Flash and Deb Smith ; a few will remember the noble horse which performed the service I have ascribed to Roger ; and the descendants of a certain family will not have forgotten some of the pranks of Joe and Jake Fairthorn."

The landscapes of " the park-like region of Kennett " are described with a richness of phrase that is heightened by the evident affection of the author for the places of his description. He misses no feature of the scene : the swelling slopes of clover and stubble-field, the blue level of Toughkenamon, the oak woods of

Avondale, the massive stone farm-houses, the walled gardens, the hedges of hawthorn and blackthorn, the young white-oak leaves on the twentieth of April the size of a squirrel's ear, the snowy pyramids of dogwood bloom, the "lush, tropical splendor of vegetation such as England never knew [which] heaped the woods and hung the roadside with sprays which grew and bloomed and wantoned, as if growth were a conscious joy rather than blind obedience to a law."

Like Plumer Ward's De Vere who had got by heart every leaf and lady in the Mall of St. James's Park, Bayard Taylor knew every feature of Chester County, from "the red umbels of the tall eupatoriums in the meadow," that announce the close of summer, to the "pink-veined bells of the muskodeed," that are prophecies of spring.

To the people of Kennett the book had a special value and interest, for it contained events that they remembered and people whom they knew. The memory of the deeds of Fitzpatrick (Sandy Flash) was still rife in Chester County minds, and searches were still instituted after his hidden treasure. Dougherty, the Irish hostler of the Unicorn tavern in the story, was actually an accomplice of Fitzpatrick, though the real place of his employment was one mile

northwest of Newtown Square at a tavern once
called Pratt's House and in the last century
kept by Benjamin West's father.[1]

"Deb" Smith, who, with a strange stirring
of a better self not altogether coerced and
strangled in her brutalized nature, befriended
and served Gilbert Potter,[2] was well known in
East Marlborough Township and the neighborhood as Rachel McMullen, and was popularly
believed to be colleagued with the highwayman.

Martha Deane, "the dear and noble woman"
whose character shines with the purest radiance,
one of the gentlest and sweetest figures in
American literature, was Ruth Baldwin, who
as the wife of Thomas Wilson lived in the vine-
covered house at the east end of Unionville.
Her grave is a short distance out of Unionville
on the road to Cedarcroft.

Bayard Taylor's grandfather is farmer Fairthorn, whose marriage, "having been a stolen
match, and not performed according to 'Friends'
ceremony,' occasioned his excommunication.
He might have been restored to the rights of
membership by admitting his sorrow for the
offense, but this he stoutly refused to do." The

---

[1] In the neighboring Seventh-Day Baptist Churchyard
some of West's family are buried, and Anthony Wayne's
mother and four of her children.

[2] Gilbert Potter's house still stands, two miles south of
Kennett.

farmhouse stood on the right of the wood immediately north of Kennett Square, "in the hollow into which the road dips, on leaving the village."

The two mischievous boys, Joe and Jake Fairthorn, are Bayard Taylor's father and uncle, though many of the pranks ascribed to them Taylor drew from the recollections of his own childhood. "The boys had been in the habit of taking the farm-horses out of the field and riding them up and down the Unionville road. It was their habit, as soon as they had climbed 'the big hill,' to use stick and voice with great energy, force the animals into a gallop, and so dash along the level. Very soon, the horses knew what was expected of them, and whenever they came abreast of the great chestnut-tree on the top of the hill, they would start off as if possessed. If any business called Farmer Fairthorn to the Street Road, or up Marlborough way, Joe and Jake, dancing with delight, would dart around the barn, gain the wooded hollow, climb the big hill behind the lime-kiln, and hide themselves under the hedge, at the commencement of the level road. Here they could watch their father, as his benign unsuspecting face came in sight, mounting the hill, either upon the gray mare, Bonnie, or the brown gelding Peter. As the horse neared the chestnut-tree, they fairly shook with eager expectancy — then came the start, the astonishment of the old man, his frantic ' Whoa, there, whoa ! ' his hat soaring off on the wind, his short stout body bouncing in the saddle, as, half unseated, he clung with one hand to the mane and the other to the bridle ! — while the wicked boys, after breathlessly watching him out of sight, rolled over and over on the grass, shrieking and yelling in a perfect luxury of fun.

"Then they knew that a test would come, and prepared themselves to meet it. When, at dinner, Farmer Fairthorn turned to his wife and said, ' Mammy,' (so he always addressed her) ' I don't know what 's the matter with Bonnie ; why, she came nigh runnin' off with me ! ' — Joe, being the oldest and boldest, would look up in well-affected surprise, and ask, ' Why, how, Daddy ? ' while Jake would bend down his head and whimper, — ' Somethin' 's got into my eye' " (p. 147). So real are the characters throughout that when they speak one almost seems to hear the " close wiry twang peculiar to Southern Pennsylvania." Miss Betsy Lavender, the all-knowing spinster whose " knowledge of farms, families, and genealogies extended up to Fallowfield on one side, and over to Birmingham on the other," is a masterpiece of character-drawing, but Taylor always denied that in this instance he had any particular person in mind.[1]

"Hannah Thurston" represented "the serious people" of Chester County; "The Story of Kennett" depicts "the old time cheer." With a sigh for the mirth that was gone, Taylor wrote in the "Proem" to "Home Pastorals:" —

"Gone are the olden cheer, the tavern-dance, and the fox-hunt,
Muster at trainings, buxom lasses that rode upon pillions;
Husking-parties and jovial home-comings after the wedding,
Gone, as they never had been! — and now, the serious people
Solemnly gather to hear some wordy itinerant speaker
Talking of Temperance, Peace, or the Right of Suffrage for
    Women."

The fox chase in Avondale Woods with which the story of Kennett begins, and the wedding with which it ends, are bold and faithful delineations of the characteristically English life of the Pennsylvanian country. The most powerful and dramatic chapter however, and that which excited most comment, is the funeral of Abiah Barton. For twenty-five years Mary Potter had been secretly married to old Barton's son Alfred, and had taken an oath not to speak of the marriage until the old man's death. For a

---

[1] Mr. Julius F. Sachse believes that the original of Betsy Lavender was Gobitha Withers, a member of St. James's Church, Marlborough, Chester County, Pa. St. James's is known as the "lost" parish. It is the only pre-revolutionary parish that has gone out of existence.

quarter of a century her lips were sealed and
the shadow of ignominy fell upon Gilbert, her
noble son. Her time of justification comes with
Barton's death and at the funeral she has *her
day*. The critics disputed her right to call it
" her day," and " to make the old man's coffin a
platform on which to exhibit her triumph or her
justification."   Mr. J. B. Phillips, a life-long
friend of Taylor, used a friend's prerogative
and expressed with uncompromising candor and
force the opinion that must be shared by many
readers of the book : " The principal person
who has my sympathy on that occasion is Gilbert Potter. He is the man that is pilloried.
For him the thing must have been perfectly
awful. I can't imagine how his worst or mean-
est enemy, by the utmost stretch of malice,
could have by any possibility contrived a more
harrowing way of breaking to him a most loath-
some fact. His humiliation is perfect and complete. I agree with him that Sandy Flash were
a much better father. I fail to see much
triumph in Mary's hanging on to Alf's rotten
carcass. The funeral becomes a rabble not
pleasant to contemplate. The procession is
broken, and men lash their horses to get ahead
and gloat their greedy eyes on the pilloried Alf
and Potter and the triumphant Mary Potter."

Taylor defended what he called the most justifiable chapter in the book by saying "she had fixed, for years, just this justification in her mind; there is a vein of superstition about her; she sees simply what she believes the Lord has directed her to do and she does it. . . . I was a year studying out the plot before I began to write, and the idea of the *dénouement* at the funeral came to me like an inspiration." Nevertheless the chapter remains a repulsive one, and the reader recoils from its horror and its shame.

The pretty scene of love-making between Gilbert Potter and Martha Deane seems to me not only the best chapter in the book but the most exquisite incident of the kind in American literature. The sylvan setting of the scene of tender and pure emotion is full of charm : —

"The long rays of sunset withdrew to the treetops, and a deeper hush fell upon the land. The road, which had mounted along the slope of a stubble - field, now dropped again into a wooded hollow, where a tree, awkwardly felled, lay across it. Roger pricked up his ears and leaped lightly over. Martha's horse followed, taking the log easily, but she reined him up the next moment, uttering a slight exclamation, and stretched out her hand wistfully towards Gilbert.

"To seize it and bring Roger to a stand was the work of an instant. 'What is the matter, Martha ?' he cried.

" ' I think the girth is broken,' said she. ' The saddle is loose, and I was nigh losing my balance. Thank you, I can sit steadily now.'

" Gilbert sprang to the ground and hastened to her assistance. ' Yes, it is broken,' he said, ' but I can give you mine. You had better dismount, though; see, I will hold the pommel firm with one hand, while I lift you down with the other. Not too fast, I am strong; place your hands on my shoulders, — so ! '

" She bent forward and laid her hands upon his shoulders. Then, as she slid gently down, his right arm crept around her waist, holding her so firmly and securely that she had left the saddle and hung in its support while her feet had not yet touched the earth. Her warm breath was on Gilbert's forehead ; her bosom swept his breast, and the arm that until then had supported, now swiftly, tenderly, irresistibly embraced her. Trembling, thrilling from head to foot, utterly unable to control the mad impulse of the moment, he drew her to his heart, and laid his lips to hers. All that he would have said — all, and more than all, that words could have expressed — was now said, without words. His kiss clung as if it were the last this side of death, — clung until he felt that Martha feebly strove to be released.

" The next minute they stood side by side, and

Gilbert, by a revulsion equally swift and over-powering, burst into a passion of tears. He turned and leaned his head against Roger's neck.

" Presently a light touch came upon his shoulder.

" ' Gilbert ! '

" He faced her then, and saw that her own cheeks were wet. ' Martha ! ' he cried, ' unless you love me with a love like mine for you, you can never forgive me ! '

" She came nearer ; she laid her arms around him, and lifted her face to his. Then she said, in a tender, tremulous whisper, —

" ' Gilbert — Gilbert ! I forgive you.' "

The fourth and last of Bayard Taylor's novels, " Joseph and his Friend : A Story of Pennsylvania," was begun in January, 1869, at Cedarcroft, contributed serially to the " Atlantic," and published by Putnam, November 24, 1870. It is an unpleasant story of mean duplicity and painful mistakes. The characters are shallow and their surroundings shabby. There is not a single pleasing situation or incident in the book. Bismarck told Bayard Taylor that he had read the novel twice and was sure that it contained one serious defect. He said, " You let your villain escape too easily ; that is not poetic justice, nor any kind of justice, in my opinion."

CHAPTER V.

1867-1874.

" THE Story of Kennett" and "The Picture of St. John" were published in 1866. The former was Bayard Taylor's best prose work, the latter his first sustained poem. Between the publication of the novel in the spring, and the poem in the fall, two summer months were spent roughing it in the Rockies.[1] Looking back across the twenty years of authorship that lay between " Views Afoot," and " The Story of Kennett," Bayard Taylor regarded the products of those years as so many phases of an education which circumstances had compelled him to acquire in the sight of the public. " In a literary sense," he wrote to J. B. Phillips, August 5, 1866, " I have almost entirely changed in the last five years."

Between his return from Europe in 1858 and

[1] *Colorado: A Summer Trip* (1867) is the narrative of this vacation.

his departure again in 1867 he had published nine volumes and given six hundred lectures. He was exhausted, and longed for rest; but he felt that his *Wanderjahre* were over, and that he had solid ground beneath his feet and a definite place in the world of letters.

He was growing vigorously and continuously. The phrase " cosmical experience," so often on his lips, was the expression of his eager joy in progress, and of the delight he felt as he wheeled into a new orbit, in exploring new lands, or encountering new lives. He craved intellectual novelty, and quieted the demands of his nervous intellect by taking up unusual studies or essaying the painter's brush in place of the pen.

His early life had been warped by sentimentality and cribbed by repression. Two centuries of Quaker ancestry had condemned him to slow development. From the first there was a purely literary strain in his blood, but the nice sense of proportion and of harmony was slowly arrived at. He was, he said, ten years behind every other American author; but when those who had the start of him flowered and ceased he was stepping on with quick impatience to more novel experiments and to more conspicuous results. The really great things of which he was capable were still before him when he died, with more unfulfilled renown and unaccomplished growth within him than any other man in American letters.

It was characteristic of such a nature, and of such an intellectual history, to regard with dissatisfaction that was sometimes almost shame the works of the earliest stages of its development. Always the last thing he did he regarded as his best. He had no interest in work behind him. The book he was writing was leagues in advance of anything he had written. He was offended, or at least hurt, when in answer to the question he so frequently put to his friends, — " Which book of mine do you like the best ? " — one said " Poems of the Orient " and another "John Godfrey's Fortunes." He was extremely sensitive to critical opinion, and innocently vain of his personal history. It was his natural and inevitable hunger for recognition and sympathy that made him repeat with keen enjoyment the favorable words of men whom he respected.

After the Civil War, Taylor found a new set of literary men in New York ; the old order had changed, giving place to new. He began to see better work in store for him, and with splendid energy and resolution he undertook to bury his superficial, ephemeral popularity as traveler and journalist, and to acquire another and higher reputation.

About 1850 he first conceived the idea of translating " Faust." In September or October, 1863, he commenced the work; in May, 1870, he finished it. The notes were written in nine months more, and the first part was published in December, 1870, and the second part in March, 1871. " Genius," said Carlyle, " is the capacity for taking infinite pains." Only a fellow of the craft can know the all-unestimated sum of pains that went to the magnificent success of Taylor's matchless rendering of the great German poem. He toiled terribly upon it. He mastered much of the prodigious literature that has accumulated about the greatest poem of the nineteenth century. He familiarized himself with the ramifications of the legend in history and art. He examined a score of translations, read commentaries, compared sundry editions, and compressed the labor of a lifetime into seven years. The learned world at first mistrusted him, the task seemed so impossible; but with the completion of the work all doubts and distrust were lost in the universal appreciation and acceptance of the splendid achievement.

Bayard Taylor's education had come largely from travel. He picked his knowledge from the living bush. He was not a learned man ; indeed he was notoriously no scholar. He was not sure of the correctness of the Latin title of his poem, "Notus Ignoto." He was fifty, as has been already noted, before he took up the study of Greek. He was, however, a close and rapid reader, and had a tenacious memory that dropped not a single thread. After the lapse of twenty or thirty years he could still promptly recall poems that he had committed to memory in his youth. Indeed, his memory was sometimes a thwart disnatured torment to him, when some wretched doggerel that he had read once and incontinently rejected arose in his recollection after a score of years with distressing distinctness. He knew by heart the entire First Part of Faust and most of the Second; and he frequently made his translation from the ring of the original in his ear and not from a perusal of the printed page.

The great world of eye and ear had taught him more than it vouchsafes to most men who lift its jealous veils. He had a wide knowledge of men and affairs that spread a far horizon about his literary work. He had lived and looked about him. He was once surprised at Cedarcroft with an order from the "Tribune" to prepare a sketch of Louis Napoleon "to be used in the event of the emperor's abdication." Drawing almost entirely from the stores of his memory, Taylor wrote in three days an entire page of the "Tribune."

It is doubtful if any foreigner ever obtained more complete mastery than Bayard Taylor of the resources of the German language. At Vienna, when he was reporting the Exhibition of 1873 for the "New York Tribune," in an impromptu speech at the journalists' banquet he coined a new and felicitous German word, — *Weltgemüthlichkeit*, — which was received with approbation and was made the title of a leading article in one of the Viennese dailies.

His German style was idiomatic, his vocabulary full, and his command of the harmonies of verse extraordinarily prompt and accurate. One pretty little poem in the manner of Kotzebue has been already quoted, but as Goethe in general and "Faust" in particular were Taylor's cult, the object of his best directed energies, and as his studies in German led to his most positive and permanent literary triumphs, it seems well to illustrate a little further his skill and originality in marshaling German verse.

After the surrender of MacMahon's army Taylor wrote "Jubel-lied eines Amerikaners," which was published in "Lieder zu Schutz und Trutz" (Berlin, 1870), and republished in the "Neue Reichs-Commersbuch," edited by Müller von der Werra. It was set to music by Jakob Blied. This popular *triumph-lied* ran : —

" Triumph ! das Schwert in tapf'rer Hand
  Hat hohe That vollbracht ;
Vereint ist nun das deutsche Land
  Zum Sieg und Ruhm erwacht !
Die Macht, die jüngst so höhnisch prahlt
  Giebt auf die letzte Wehr,
Und neuer Glanz der Thaten strahlt
  Auf Deutschlands Helden heer !

" Heil edles Volk ! dem neu das Herz
  So unerschüttert schlug !
Das sich verband und allerwärts
  Verwarf den fränk'schen Trug !
Das, fest und heilig, Glied an Glied,
  Stand endlich im Verein
Mit Trost und Muth, Gebet und Lied,
  Eine einz'ge Wacht am Rhein !

" Kanonen, donnert noch einmal !
  Den Frieden nun ihr bringt :
Ihr Glocken, über Berg und Thal
  Von Tausend Thürmen klingt !
Fromm neige dich, O deutsches Land
  Lass Rache ruhn und Spott :
Dein Gott erhalf und überwand
  Nun danket Alle Gott ! "

Bayard Taylor's intellect was of that activity
that it gave him trouble not to work ; and his
superabundant animal spirits abandoned him in
his hours of relaxation to the most riotous quips
and voluntary absurdities.   At his evenings at
home in New York he and his merry comrades
played practical jokes and fantastic pranks ; and

in the " Echo Club " in frolicsome mood he trav-
estied the gravest lines of serious men.   Humor
is a severe test of a translator's skill.   Jests are
such frail atomies that they scarcely bear trans-
port from their native territory.   The gibe that
in one country makes the whole quire hold their
hips and laugh, and waxen in their mirth, appears dull and leaden unto another people.

That Taylor had acquired with the German
tongue a full appreciation of the quality of
German humor appears in the following parody
extemporized at Gotha : —

> " Kennst du das Land, wo schönste Braten blühn,
>   Im Lettichlaub die goldnen Eier glühn,
>   Ein sanfterer Duft vom Marcobrunner weht
>   Gemüse still, und hoch das Wildpret steht,
>   Kennst du es wohl ? Dahin, dahin,
>   Möcht ich, geliebte Frau, zum Essen mit dir ziehn!
>
> " Kennst du das Haus ? Gastfreundlich ist sein Dach :
>   Die Liebe wohnt im Saal und im Gemach,
>   Und edle Wirthe stehen und sehen uns an :
>   Was haben sie schon oft so viel für uns gethan !
>   Kennst du es wohl ? Dahin, dahin,
>   Möcht wieder ich mit der Familie ziehn!
>
> " Kennst du den Berg und seinen Gartensteg ?
>   Durch Himbeersträuch die Gäste ziehen ihren Weg,
>   Doch oben wohnt das theure edle Paar,
>   Die uns bewirthet schon so manches Jahr,
>   Kennst du sie wohl ? Dahin, dahin,
>   So oft sie rufen, woll'n wir Alle ziehn."

In his translation of " Faust " Taylor aimed
to reproduce the rhythm, the oral effect of the
original, no less than its logical or grammatical
meaning. Enamored of his toil, and thrilled
with the mighty melody of the verse, he conceived the lines " An Goethe " which stand at
the front of his translation. They seem to me
resplendent with gleams that are kindred to the
great spirit with whom Taylor had held such
close and high converse : —

> " Erhabener Geist, im Geisterreich verloren !
> Wo immer Deine lichte Wohnung sey,
> Zum höh'ren Schaffen bist Du neugeboren,
> Und singest dort die voll're Litanei.
> Von jenem Streben das Du auserkoren,
> Vom reinsten Aether, drin Du athmest frei,
> O neige Dich zu gnädigem Erwiedern
> Des letzten Wiederhalls von Deinen Liedern !

> " Den alten Musen die bestäubten Kronen
> Nahmst Du, zu neuem Glanz, mit kühner Hand :
> Du löst die Räthsel ältester Aeonen
> Durch jüngeren Glauben, helleren Verstand,
> Und machst, wo rege Menschengeister wohnen,
> Die ganze Erde Dir zum Vaterland ;
> Und Deine Jünger sehn in Dir, verwundert,
> Verkörpert schon das werdende Jahrhundert.

> " Was Du gesungen, Aller Lust und Klagen,
> Des Lebens Wiedersprüche, neu vermählt, —
> Die Harfe tausendstimmig frisch geschlagen,
> Die Shakspeare einst, die einst Homer gewählt —
> Darf ich in fremde Klänge übertragen
> Das Alles, wo so Mancher schon gefehlt ?

Lass Deinen Geist in meiner Stimme klingen,
Und was Du sangst, lass mich es Dir nachsingen! "

Concerning these verses, which moult no
feather in comparison with Goethe's own, Taylor wrote to Professor James Morgan Hart :
" It would be impossible for me to translate
my own German proem, because it was conceived in German. I could only give the same
thought, in English — although *my own* — in
paler colors."

The translation of " Faust " was not done in
leisure or without interruption. The hope of
reducing his expenses, and the pleasant anticipation of meeting old friends and family con-
nections in Germany, led Taylor, in February,
1867, to sail for Europe. Rest was his intention, but the necessity of providing for the
expenses of Cedarcroft compelled him to write
a number of letters to the " Tribune," and
articles for the " Atlantic Monthly."

From England, where he met several men of
letters, he went to Gotha, and then to Lausanne.
He did considerable painting in both oil and
water colors, and he made two trips, one to " the
little land of Appenzell," and one to Paris to see
the International Exhibition. His letters to the
" Tribune " related chiefly to the art collections
of the exhibition, and his judgments upon the
American works were at once candid and kind.

At the close of May he started for Spain intending to visit some out of the way places of Europe. The first of the " Atlantic " papers that record this journey is " From Perpignan to Montserrat." He has written few better descriptions than that of the serrated mountain, the " strange, solitary, exiled peak, drifted away in the beginning of things from its brethren of the Pyrenees." No doubt his chief interest in it was because Goethe had appropriated the scenery of Montserrat for the fifth act of the second part of " Faust."

He made one excursion to the Balearic Islands, another over Catalonian bridle-roads to the little republic of Andorra in the Pyrenees, undisturbed by the changes of a thousand years of history. He was the first American who ever saw this forgotten corner, which is probably even now known only through Halévy's opera " Le Val d'Andorre."

He returned to Lausanne and Gotha by way of the Grande Chartreuse and the Château Bayard. He rested during July and August at Friedrichrode, where he, together with James Lorimer Graham, had taken a villa. " Our cottage," he wrote to Mr. Stedman, " has a flagstaff, and on that staff floats the American flag; inside we have German lessons, exercises in art, beer, wine, occasional trout, visitors from

Gotha, chess, and my papers for the 'Atlantic.'"

After a little visiting among friends and relatives, and an excursion to Kyffhäuser (for its legends of Barbarossa), Taylor and his party turned southward again over the Brenner Pass into Italy. He became ill at Verona, but pushed on to Venice where the travelers halted for a while, and Taylor, sketching by the canal, became poisoned with malaria and rapidly developed the latent fever in his system. Fortunately the party reached Florence before the illness culminated, and, in Casa Guidi, he lay in delirium for four weeks. His strong constitution, the wise services of his English physician, and the sedulous care of those about him saved his life. After his recovery he wrote a poem, suggested by the circumstance that in the house in which he had been nursed back to life Elizabeth Barrett Browning had once lived, and written some of her most memorable verse, and died; and he sent the poem to Robert Browning.

> " Returned to warm existence, — even as one
> Sentenced, then blotted from the headsman's book,
> Accepts with doubt the life again begun, —
> I leave the duress of my couch, and look
> Through Casa Guidi windows to the sun.
>
> • • • • • • • • • • • •

" She came, whom Casa Guidi chambers knew,
   And know more proudly, an Immortal, now ;
   The air without a star was shivered through
   With the resistless radiance of her brow,
   And glimmering landscapes from the darkness grew.

" Thin, phantom-like ; and yet she brought me rest.
   Unspoken words, an understood command,
   Sealed weary lids with sleep, together pressed
   In clasping quiet wandering hand to hand,
   And smoothed the folded cloth above the breast.
   . . . .

" The tablet tells you, ' Here she wrote and died,'
   And grateful Florence bids the record stand :
   Here bend Italian love and English pride
   Above her grave, — and one remoter land,
   Free as her prayers would make it, at their side."

After his convalescence he spent a month
(January, 1868) in Naples, living on the quay
of Santa Lucia from which he moved just in
time, for he had been gone but four days when
the great rock of Pizzofalcone behind the quay
fell, demolishing among others the house in
which he had lived and killing eighty persons.
" Atlantic " papers, " A Week on Capri " and
" A Trip to Ischia," were written in February
at Sorrento.   In March he arrived in Rome,
where he spent two months with Buchanan Read
and Bierstadt and troops of friends ; he engaged
a studio and spent the forenoons figure-painting.
After a brief sojourn in Florence, in the old
quarters at Casa Guidi, he made an excursion to

Corsica and the Island of Maddalena, where he had " a distant view of Caprera," as Garibaldi declined to see him.

In September, 1868, he returned to America and to Cedarcroft. He celebrated the golden wedding of his parents with a week of mirth and frolic. Health seemed to be held in the Taylor family by tenure of gavelkind ; three generations in succession had celebrated their golden wedding. Boker and Stoddard, who on this occasion were present, read poems, and Taylor composed a pretty little masque in the pleasant ancient manner.

The year 1869 was spent almost entirely at Cedarcroft. It began with the writing of " Notus Ignoto " and ended with the approaching completion of " Faust." The arduous studies for the latter work were made more toilsome by the distraction of the " Gettysburg Ode." The great significance of the dedication of the monument at Gettysburg, and his own personal associations with that fatal field on which his brother fell, prompted him to the most painful care in the performance of what was always an uncongenial and difficult task to him, — the making of a poem of which he had not had at first the vision in his own imagination. Soon after the reading of the " Ode " at Gettysburg he was called upon to deliver the oration at Guilford,

Connecticut, upon the dedication of the granite obelisk erected in honor of Fitz-Greene Halleck, — the first public monument raised to an American poet. Nor was this all; in Ripley's absence from the "Tribune" Taylor prepared in his stead many important book reviews. He saw a new edition of "Views Afoot" through the press, and published "By-Ways of Europe." He also voluntarily interrupted his German studies to write "An August Pastoral," in which his love of the scenery and his notion of the life of his native place find a higher literary expression than in his novels.

"Therefore be still, thou yearning voice from the garden in
    Jena,
Still, thou answering voice from the park-side cottage in
    Weimar,
Still, sentimental echo from chambers of office in Dres-
    den, —
Ye, and the feebler and farther voices that sound in the
    pauses!
Each and all to the shelves I return: for vain is your com-
    merce
Now, when the world and the brain are numb in the torpor of
    August."

Taylor's "Faust" was to be published by Fields, Osgood & Co. in a volume uniform with the quarto editions of Longfellow's "Dante," and Bryant's "Iliad." Such companionship put Taylor on his mettle. A large edition appeared December 14, 1870, and nearly all the copies were sold upon that day. In the evening, at the home of James T. Fields, a small but distinguished company met to congratulate the successful translator. Longfellow, Lowell, Holmes, Howells, Aldrich, and Osgood sat around a bust of Goethe which was placed upon the library table, and the night was dedicated to Goethe and to Taylor. Whittier, who could not be present, sent a letter of regret in which he noted with fondly partial pride that " the best translation of Tasso is that of the Quaker Wiffin, and now we have the best of Goethe from the Quaker-born Taylor."

George Bancroft, at that time minister to Germany, took charge of the copies that were sent to Berlin for distribution, and almost the first copy presented in Germany was to Bismarck, who had expressed a desire to have the translation.

It was Taylor's belief that poetry absolutely required for its successful translation the original metres. And in the original metre he rendered " Faust." The merits of his version, it has been said, are sympathetic quality, rapid poetic handling, and fidelity to text. The translation of the " astonishing chorus " of the archangels with its " planetary cosmic harmony " has never been surpassed in English except by Shelley's almost inspired version. Over every

word of " Faust " Bayard Taylor pondered with
the minutest care.   Twenty or thirty synonyms
for every chief word in a quatrain were hunted
up, and hours, days, and weeks spent in making
the crooked words lie smooth.   He was right
when he said that the resonance of the original
can only be preserved when the measure is
clearly marked and the vowel harmonies imitated.

Frederick Harrison deplores that Coleridge
did not act upon Shelley's suggestion and give
us " Faust " in the language of " Wallenstein,"
" Kubla Khan," and " Christabel."   True, great
poets, of imagination all compact, with poetic
intuition have interpreted the wonderful atmosphere which envelops great poems and which
seems to defy all attempts at translation.   Yet
even Shelley, who had for years studied and
imitated the archangels' chorus, and had declared that " the volatile strength and delicacy
of the ideas escape in the crucible of translation," has but little surpassed Taylor in these
particular lines.   In the prologue to " Hellas "
Shelley had imitated the chorus ; and one year
later (1822) he attempted both a literal and
poetic translation of Goethe's lines.   Where
Shelley has, as it seems to me, far excelled Taylor is in the mocking irreverence of Mephis-
topheles.   He has caught the spirit of the lines

> " Von Zeit zu Zeit seh' ich *den Alten* gern,
>   Und hüte mich mit ihm zu brechen.
> Es ist gar hübsch von einem grossen Herrn,
>   So menschlich mit dem Teufel selbst zu sprechen,"

which he renders,

> " From time to time I visit *the old fellow*,
>   And I take care to keep on good terms with him.
> Civil enough is the same God Almighty
>   To talk so freely with the Devil himself."

How much more appropriate is this jaunty irreverence than Bayard Taylor's sedate —

> "I like at times to hear *the Ancient's word*,
>   And have a care to be most civil:
> It 's really kind of such a noble Lord
>   So humanly to gossip with the Devil."

September 2, 1869, Bayard Taylor accepted his election to the non-resident professorship of German literature at Cornell University. In the spring of the following year, April 20–May 2, he delivered a course of lectures before the university upon Lessing, Klopstock, Schiller, Goethe, and Humboldt. In order that the citizens of Ithaca, as well as the students, might attend, the lectures were given in Library Hall.

The following year Taylor wrote new lectures upon the earliest German literature, the Minnesingers, the Mediæval Epic, the Nibelungenlied, the literature of the Reformation, and the literature of the seventeenth century. These were read in Ithaca, in June, 1871, and repeated May

21–29, 1877. In May, 1875, he lectured upon Lessing, Klopstock, Herder, Wieland, Richter, Schiller, and Goethe. Many warm friendships began between the lecturer and members of the faculty of Cornell University; Goldwin Smith "carried away a pleasant memory of his pleasant lectures," and from Professor Willard Fiske and Professor W. T. Hewett, Taylor received scholarly suggestions that his quick brain wrought into fresh material for literary fame and profit.

A cough which had been troublesome through the winter of 1869–1870, and caused some concern to his friends, clung to him so persistently that in May, 1870, he started for California, hoping not only to regain his wonted health, but to earn by lecturing some much needed money. Every anticipation was disappointed, and he returned home, confessing a loss of several hundred dollars.

It is unfortunate that the lives of authors should come to be sordid or shabby histories of financial distress, — mere records of getting and spending. The French, with justice, censure English biography for the perpetual presence in it of the guinea's stamp. But in the story of Taylor's life it seems inevitable that his biographer should refer frequently to his business vicissitudes, for Taylor's life was a struggle for the means to live, and the intensity of the struggle is the measure of the difficulties that beset those who in America made literature their profession.

Throughout 1871 he was continually battling against ill-health. He published the second part of "Faust," a story in the "Atlantic Monthly," a paper on Humboldt and "Down the Eastern Shore," in "Harper's Weekly," two articles for "Scribner's Magazine" and one for the "Independent." He began his editorial work upon the "Library of Travel" for Scribners, and furnished frequent articles and reviews for the "New York Tribune." He made two excursions, one to the eastern shore of Maryland, which he described in a magazine article for "Harper's," and the other to Lakes Superior and Winnipeg, with Whitelaw Reid and a party of editors, which he wrote about in letters to the "Tribune." It is not work that kills, but worry, and the cares of Cedarcroft were weighing heavily upon him. The crops failed, the cost of living increased, his own income was diminishing; debts accumulated and added to the nagging of the neighbors at Kennett. Debt is always more harshly considered in the country than in cities, and particularly so among the Quakers, who are rigidly exact and prompt in the settlement of money transactions. He had outlived the sentiment that attached him to the spot. "Seclusion in our country," he said, "means nothing but moral and intellectual stagnation." He saw the life of peace and poetry that he had dreamed of, receding from him. He realized that his move to Kennett had been a mistake, and in heavy disappointment he resolved to withdraw forever from the place. This meant a revising and recasting of his plan of life. He put Cedarcroft in the hands of an agent and offered it for sale. He went to New York, and in comfortable quarters at 12 University Place passed the winter.

The next year, 1872, he made another radical move in life. He was worn with much labor, fatigued and worried. He found that the new works of real literary merit upon which he had been for seven years engaged did not appeal to the masses; they were caviare to the general. The books of travel which he had written in his salad days he could not look into without wincing with a feeling of positive pain; yet for these books of immature intellect, and at times flippant style, he had received splendid remuneration, while from the serious and toilsome products of his ripe age, with their due proportion and developed art, he had now to be content with the most meagre profits. Not at any time did he stand more in need of money than now.

Lecturing was no longer a successful occupation, nor was it to be entered upon without
actual hazard of health. The capital invested
in his country property was unproductive. The
"Tribune" undertook a building enterprise
which absorbed its funds, and the last dividend
upon the shares that Taylor held was paid in
the spring of 1872.

The need of rest and the desire to collect
materials for the lives of Goethe and Schiller,
which it had already become his ambition to
write, determined him to go to Germany, and
to remain there for one or two years. Cedarcroft was leased in three parts; all his personal
property was placed in storage, and the old parents were comfortably established in a house in
Kennett. Taylor left his home of twelve years
never to return to it save as a visitor, and sailed
June 6, 1872, upon the steamer Westphalia for
Hamburg. The autumn he spent in the Thü-
ringerwald; in Gotha he lived at the observatory
at the corner of the park. The close of the
year brought him the news of Horace Greeley's
death, and the "Tribune's" misfortune; although he did not yet know it, he was to receive
during the remainder of his life no dividend
upon his "Tribune" shares. The only ray of
consolation for all the blackness that surrounded
him was the generous and ample recognition in

Germany of his translation of "Faust." Everywhere he came upon materials for his life of Goethe which kindled him with new eagerness and curiosity. At Ilmenau he was put into the room where Goethe celebrated his last birthday in 1831. At Rudolstadt, in July, 1872, he rambled along the paths which Schiller had followed ; he visited the forge where Schiller studied the *staffage* for his ballad of "Fridolin," and "The Song of the Bell," but was too late to see the lodge on the Kickelhahn, destroyed by fire eighteen months before, where Goethe wrote upon the wall, "Ueber allen Gipfeln ist Ruh." The Grand-Duke of Saxe-Weimar, grandson of Carl August, invited Taylor, in October, to dinner in the *Sängersaal* in the Wartburg. The dinner was served in "the same old Byzantine hall where Tannhäuser sang," between the pillars "against which certainly must have leaned Wolfram von Eschenbach and Walther von der Vogelweide."

December 12, 1872, at Gotha he lectured in German upon American literature for the benefit of the *Frauenverein.* "I have written it directly in German," he wrote to his friend Professor Hart, "but have no idea how I shall succeed in the delivery, as I have never before tried such a thing." The lecture was repeated in Weimar upon the invitation of Wieland's granddaughter, before the Gustav-Adolf Verein. It was given in the hall of the mediæval society of Arquebusiers. After the lecture the Grand-Duke said to Taylor, " You have made one serious omission; you have said nothing about yourself." The whole court was present on this occasion; and among Taylor's auditors were the grandchildren of Carl August, Goethe, Schiller, Herder, and Wieland.

At Weimar Taylor became acquainted with Baron von Stein, grandson of Frau von Stein, Baron von Gleichen-Russwurm, Schiller's grandson, the painter Preller, a protégé of Goethe whose son died in his arms, and the scholar Schöll, chief librarian at Weimar. "My great encouragement," he wrote, "is that after testing my own conception of Goethe here, by those who knew him, I am not obliged to make any change." He visited Staatsrath Stichling, the grandson of Herder, made a most interesting acquaintance in Wolfgang von Goethe, another in Herr von Salis, and yet another in Fräulein Frommann, the foster-sister of Minna Herzlieb, the "Ottilie" of Goethe's "Wahlverwandt-schaften." "Yesterday I met," he wrote, November 12, 1873, to Professor Hart, "the daughter of Falk, and so it goes, — every day the grand old time comes nearer to me through those who partly lived in it."

When he first called upon Preller he saw in the artist's room a cast of Trippel's bust of Goethe, the Apollo head, modeled in Rome in 1787. Taylor said, "I see the same head of Goethe here, and in the same position, as in my own room at home; only opposite, I have placed the Venus of Milo. He, as man, should stand beside her, as woman." Preller arose, seized Taylor by the arm, and pointed to a bust of the Venus of Milo. "There she is," he exclaimed, "I see her every day of my life, but I never pass her without saying to myself: 'My God, how beautiful she is!'"

Taylor's enthusiasm ran high, rich stores of materials were opening before him, and already the dual biography of Goethe and Schiller was taking form in his imagination. It is a little curious that his own intellectual life had followed the course of Goethe's. Like him he had begun his German life in Frankfurt, and now it was culminating with him in Weimar. The "Westoestlicher Divan" had perhaps exerted some influence over him when he was writing "Poems of the Orient;" now it was his ambition to give to American literature a poem in the style of "Faust" or "Pandora." Goethe had become his one intense literary passion!

Dogged by ill-fortune and suffering ill-health, Taylor sought the softer air of Italy, in January, 1873, resting on the way at Lausanne. He resumed his old quarters in Florence at Casa Guidi. He reported the exposition at Vienna for the "Tribune," and in summing up the literary achievement of the twelvemonth he wrote, " This is perhaps the most fruitful — certainly the most laborious — year of my life." In Lausanne, January, 1873, he began a school history of Germany for Messrs. Appleton — a potboiler by which he expected speedily to earn two or three thousand dollars. He continued the work in Florence, Gotha, and Vienna, and finished it on the first of August. In October and November he wrote " The Prophet," a play. That he was still oppressed by financial embarrassment is clear from the following letter to William D. Howells : —

GOTHA, GERMANY, *February* 6, 1874.

MY DEAR HOWELLS, — Your very welcome letter was forwarded to me from Florence three days ago. We were just ready to leave here, the first week in January, when my daughter was suddenly taken down with a severe attack of fever, from which she is now slowly recovering. We have had a month of anxiety, of waiting and watching, instead of a sunny Italian month of rest ; but we must be grateful and hopeful. I hope to get away in four or five days more.

Herewith I send you a short story, which is hardly included in our bargain, but inasmuch as short stories with meanings in them are not very abundant in the market, I conjecture that you may be willing to get it. I began an article on Weimar, but Lilian's fever interrupted me, and the fleeting fancy of the story thrust itself between. The money for it is needed in Pennsylvania ; so please have it sent as soon as possible, to my mother, Mrs. Rebecca W. Taylor, Kennett Square, Pennsylvania, and you will greatly oblige me.

I am glad you did not misinterpret the spirit of my letter. I have told you (more than once, I fancy) that I am engaged in the somewhat desperate task of burying such reputation as I had ten years ago several thousand fathoms deep, and creating a new one. I have always felt that you cordially recognized this endeavor, but the words in which you now say it are like an additional prop thrust under my will and patience. The fact that you returned the poem which I consider much the more important and original of the two was a little discouraging, coming, as it did, upon the heels of two months of steady bad news of every possible kind. I see no American papers, I do not know how my articles are received, and may, therefore, underestimate the standing I have already gained

with such men as yourself. As for the super-
cilious fashion in which I am treated by many
newspaper writers, it has long ceased to be an
annoyance.

I gladly accept your offer for four articles.
It leaves me a certain amount of freedom, which
I always need, in order to work satisfactorily.
As for poems, I confess I am still a little puz-
zled how to decide what you are likely to like
in mine. A man's taste is much more difficult
to understand than his character. However, I 'll
try again when the next one comes. I feel more
at home in the " Atlantic " than anywhere else.

My situation is a little difficult. I may tell
you *now*, that for two years past I have had no
income from my few " Tribune " shares, shall
have none for two more to come, and am now
devouring the last of the proceeds of one which
I was forced to sell. Except a pittance of about
750 dollars a year from *all* my books, I have no
income at all, except my immediate earnings,
and nearly all my labor for eighteen months past
is not yet remunerative. For instance, I spent
eight months of last year, averaging eight hours
a day, on a history of Germany for schools,
which Appletons' have not yet brought out.
Under all these restrictions, I dare not neglect
the more important Goethe studies, and when
they are finished I shall hasten home to work

for a living until the better time comes. There has been an unusual mental, moral, and physical strain upon me ever since leaving home, and a cheery word from a friend never had such a value as now. . . . Good luck to the "Atlantic," under H. and H. !

Ever faithfully yours,
BAYARD TAYLOR.

The History of Germany was based on Müller's large work, and upon Dittmar and von Rochau, and while accurate and comprehensive, was not condensed with particular originality or skill, and was scarcely available for the school use for which it was intended. Appleton & Co. found it unsatisfactory so far as the illustrations were concerned, and publication was deferred until the close of 1874, to the great disappointment of the author. Another disappointment was the English edition of "Lars : A Pastoral of Norway." It was the first of Taylor's poems to be published in England, and the sale was just one hundred and eight copies.

February, March, and April, 1874, Bayard Taylor and his family spent in an excursion to Italy and to Cairo. He wrote eleven letters from Egypt to the "Tribune." He made the acquaintance of Mariette Bey and studied with delight the new discoveries in Egyptology.

After his return to Germany he went to Leipzig
to avail himself of Hirzel's invitation to ex-
amine his unique Goethe and Schiller library.
While turning over these volumes, examining
eighteen folio scrapbooks of newspaper articles
concerning Goethe, and making notes to bear
away with him to America, an urgent request
was received from Whitelaw Reid to go to Iceland as the representative of the " Tribune " to
report the commemoration of the millennial anniversary of the first settlement of the island.
He controlled his impatience to return home,
saying that " to the few who have never known
any other *Alma Mater* than the 'New York
Tribune'

> " ('Stern rugged nurse, thy rigid lore
> With patience many a year I bore ! ')

her (or its) call is like that of the trumpet unto
the war-horse." He made the journey to Iceland in company with Cyrus Field, Murat Hal-
stead, Dr. I. I. Hayes, one of Mr. Gladstone's
sons, and Professor Magnusson, upon a steamer
that had been chartered by Mr. Field.

On the way from Edinburgh — where he
was entertained by Mr. Nelson in his magnificent home " Hope Park, " at the foot of Arthur's Seat — to Aberdeen, Taylor looked forth
upon Ury, famed in Whittier's ballad, where
once lived Robert Barclay, the Apologist, and

which in 1874 was the home of Alexander Baird. A few days later Taylor was sailing through the straits between Pomona and Shapinshay, — from which latter little island Washington Irving's father had emigrated, — and on through " desolate rainy seas " to Iceland.

Taylor was profoundly interested in all that he saw. " If you step on a blossom," he wrote in " Egypt and Iceland," " it may be an Arctic plant, unknown elsewhere; if a bird flies overhead it is probably an eider duck; if a boy speaks in the street, he may use words made venerable in the Eddas of Saemund and Snorre Sturlesson " (p. 206).

At Reikiavik Taylor presented a poem — " America to Iceland " — which was immediately translated into Icelandic by Mathias Jochumsson, the translator of " Lear " and " Macbeth." Taylor in turn Englished Magnusson's Icelandic address to King Christian IX.

His farewell reflections upon Iceland were : " Not Thingvalla, or Hekla, or the Geysers, — not the desolate fire-blackened mountains, the awful gloom of the dead lava plains, the bright lakes and majestic fiords, — have repaid me for the journey, but the brief glimpse of a grand and true-hearted people, innocent children in their trust and their affection, almost more than men in their brave unmurmuring endurance ! "

The Iceland trip postponed Taylor's return to America for a month; it was not until September 9, 1874, that he arrived in New York. He brought home with him a considerable library containing many rare and valuable books upon Goethe and Schiller. He went at once to Cedarcroft, where he was a guest of his own family, and set about a mountain of work. He put in order the letters he had sent to the "Tribune" and published them in October under the title "Egypt and Iceland;" he wrote the first of his papers on Weimar for the "Atlantic Monthly;" many invitations to lecture were accepted, and a new lecture, "Ancient Egypt," was prepared; an immense correspondence was dispatched, and above all the distractions of the moment and brightening over the mass of toil that filled his busy hours, shone the alluring prospect of the new Life of Goethe. " My one great encouragement since coming here," Taylor had written from Weimar, " is the assurance that I have nothing to unlearn. My *auffassung* of Goethe, as man and poet, in every important point is confirmed by those who knew him personally." The chief encouragement after his return was the cordial recognition of the merit of his literary work, and most of all the simple but sincere welcome which he received within three months of his fiftieth year from his Chester County friends and neighbors at Mount Cuba, the scene of some of the incidents of " Lars." The spontaneity and simplicity of the greeting, the soft air and tender pastoral landscape, wiped from his mind many rude memories of the conflicts of opinion and habit that the jarring years had written there, and he thanked God and took courage, facing bravely the new work that was to build for him the reputation that he still yearned for in the highest courts of literature.

Another recognition, too, he appreciated highly. Upon the invitation of the Delta Kappa Epsilon fraternity he acted as chairman of their national convention at the University of Virginia and delivered an oration.

CHAPTER VI.

POEMS AND PLAYS.

BAYARD TAYLOR was never more delighted than when in Iceland he was called " the American Skald." Nothing kindled his pride and his pleasure like praise of his poetry. His fame as a traveler and a journalist, however wide and secure, was slightly weighed by him; and the superficial repute that came with lecturing and with editing brought him regret rather than satisfaction. The laurels he coveted were far other than these. In his inmost heart, nourishing his wonderful vitality, burned a sacred and unquenchable ambition to bear the name of Poet, and to be reckoned with those great singers who have flashed the torch of spiritual life above the throngs of men. All other efforts and aspirations were subordinated to this absorbing passion. No praise of his miscellaneous achievements, when he was winning and wearing proud distinction in statecraft, in scholarship, and in letters, could reconcile him to the slightest sense of failure in his poetic endeavor. He toiled terribly, he exhausted himself with the multitude

of his tasks, "he wore himself out and perished
prematurely of hard and sometimes bitter work."
The recompense was in the sweet silent hours —
"the holy hours," as Klopstock called them —
dedicated to poetry. He was saved from the
cynicism and hardness that are often the consequence of such companionship and such toil as
were sometimes his in New York, not only by
the sweetness and gentleness of his disposition
but by the refreshing and purifying influence
of his single-hearted devotion to the highest
poetry. George Henry Boker well says : " His
childlike purity and joyousness of heart he owed
to the worship of an art for which his reverence
was boundless. . . . He believed himself to be
a poet, — of what stature and quality it is now
for the world to decide, — and in that faith he
wrought at his vocation with an assiduity and a
careful husbanding of his time and opportuni-
ties for mental and for written poetical composition, that was wonderful as an exhibition of
human industry, and in its many and varied results, when we take into consideration his wandering life and his diversified and exacting em-
ployments."

The passion to be remembered with those who
in song have lent a glory to the language we
inherit, was the inspiration and the disappointment of his life. It was with a smile that had a

touch of sadness in it that he told of his encounter with a stranger who asked permission to
take him by the hand, saying that he had read
and enjoyed all his books.

"And what do you think of my poetry?"
asked Taylor.

"Poetry," was the astonished reply, "did you
ever write any poetry?"

We have seen how with trembling hesitation
he addressed a copy of his first, frail volume of
collected verses to Longfellow, and another to
Lowell, hardly daring to hope, in his boyish
phrase, that he might call himself "a brother-
bard." Once when alone in Lowell's library, he
came upon a copy of his translation of "Faust"
lying idly, with the leaves uncut, upon the shelf,
and his sensitive nature sustained an instant
wound, to which no philosophy could make
him indifferent.

The fellow craftsman's sympathy he longed
for, and was at his best when in the company
of poets. After reading Poe's criticism upon
Tennyson, he eagerly sought for the volume, and
the mature man, recalling the raptures of the
lad of seventeen, wrote, "I remember also the
strange sense of mental dazzle and bewilderment
I experienced on the first perusal of it. I can
only compare it to the first sight of a sunlit landscape through a prism: every object has a rain-

bowed outline. One is fascinated to look again and again, though the eyes ache."

Twenty-five years after that first looking into Tennyson, Bayard Taylor spent a long day at Farringford with the Laureate. He was shown a great stretch of wheat-fields bought by " Enoch Arden ; " he was treated to Napoleon's port and to bumpers of rich brown sherry, out of magnums, thirty years old, — " meant to be drunk by Cleopatra or Catherine of Russia," said Tennyson. He heard the Laureate read " Guinevere," in " a strange monotonous chant with unexpected falling inflections," and essay the difficult " Boadicea," " chanting the lumbering lines with great unction." Mrs. Browning says, that

" Poets ever fail in reading their own verses to the worth,
The chariot wheels jar in the gates thro' which they drive
    them forth."

Tennyson read his " Idylls of the King " with choral intonation, for he was completely dominated by the metrical sense. He read for " atmosphere," letting the intellectual articulation take care of itself. Bayard Taylor read for the " sense ; " all that he did was done, as Bacon would have said, " in dry light." The spiritual man in Tennyson moulded and informed his verse ; with Taylor the verse was built up by intellectual intention.

Soon after the visit or visitation, to Tennyson,

Taylor called upon Matthew Arnold, whose appearance immediately reminded him of George William Curtis, and upon Robert Browning, on whose table he found " The Picture of St. John." To Swinburne, Taylor read his " Sunshine of the Gods : " —

> " Be glad, for this is the token,
>   The sign and the seal of the Poet;
> Were it held by will or endeavor,
>   There were naught so precious in Song.
> Wait : for the shadows unlifted
> To a million that crave the sunshine,
> Shall be lifted for thee erelong.
> Light from the loftier regions
> Here unattainable ever, —
> Bath of brightness and beauty, —
> Let it make thee glad and strong !
> Not to clamor or fury,
> Not to lament or yearning,
> But to faith and patience cometh
> The Sunshine of the Gods,
> The hour of perfect Song ! " —

and elicited the criticism that the poem should either contain more rhyme or none at all. He profited by the advice of the master of harmonies, as he had profited by the lessons of life — his hard task-master — and rested humbly proud that to his faith and patience had come, not once, but often, in soft subordination, " the Sunshine of the Gods, the hour of perfect Song," admitting him to the choice companionship of those whose fame he had reverenced and followed afar off.

How in early childhood he began to make verses, and to enjoy the " airy ecstasy " of imagination, and to feel " the first delicious thrills of faith and pride " has been already told. His earliest incentive to poetry he has analyzed in " The Picture of St. John."

> " Our state was humble, — yet above the dust,
>   If deep below the stars, — the state that feeds
>   Impatience, hinting yet denying needs,
>   And thus, on one side ever forward thrust
>   And on the other cruelly repressed,
>   My nature grew, — a wild-flower in the weeds, —
>   And hurt by ignorant love, that fain had blessed,
>   I sought some other bliss wherein to rest."

The first timid collection of his poems, " Ximena, or the Battle of the Sierra Morena, and other Poems," now an extremely rare volume, is imitative and not indicative of unusual promise.

The " Rhymes of Travel, Ballads and Poems," published in December, 1848, was approvingly criticised by Edgar Allan Poe. The qualities which Poe found in " The Continents," glowing imagination and " sonorous well-balanced rhythm," are precisely the merits of Taylor's maturest verse. In his " Epistle from Mount Tmolus " Taylor refers to

> " The curse
>   Or blessing, which has clung to me from birth —
>   The torment and the ecstasy of verse."

In his youth he coveted the flash and glitter of
rhetoric, with little consideration for the sub-
stance of poetry. The people of America had
then what Charles Lamb called "the *album*inous
fever." Annuals containing pretty poems were
cherished by the household; newspapers had
their poet's corner for artificial sentiment;
commonplace books were filled with select
stanzas and favorite fancies from Rufus Dawes,
and Grenville Mellen, and Brainard, and Sands,
admiringly bayoneted with exclamation marks.
The prevailing sentimentality is in the titles of
the approved books of 1840 : "Mildred's Lovers," "The Jar of Honey, and other Poems."
Bayard Taylor began in this environment, and
beat his way out of the wilderness to symmetrical conceptions and proportioned Art.

From 1849 to 1852, Bayard Taylor was reveling in the delight of the intellect, and writing
poems in a furor. The first adequate measure
of his lyrical power was "A Book of Romances,
Lyrics and Songs," which appeared in 1851. The
longest poem in the collection, "Mon-da-min,
or the Romance of Maize," is drawn, like Hia-
watha, from Schoolcraft. Here, too, "Hylas "
is found, the best of Taylor's classical poems,
and worthy to stand beside all but the best of
Walter Savage Landor. Two Eastern poems
prelude "the full meridian deluge " of the

" Poems of the Orient." Both these, " Kubleh," and " The Soldier and the Pard," illustrate Taylor's skill in narrative verse and his love for all animal creation. " Hassan to his Mare " and the capital ballad " Eric and Axel " are among the finest poems on the horse that our literature contains.

Taylor makes his Lars say,

> " The honest things
> Like him that likes them, over all the world."

and the poor creatures of earth seemed to be attracted to Taylor in the same way that men were.

" The Poems of the Orient " (1854) is the highest expression of Taylor's delight in the world. It contains the best of his lyrical genius, and the most brilliant of his purely sensuous verse. It was his custom to copy his poems for the printer. The neatly written and faultless manuscripts that he furnished to his publishers have misled some of his critics into thinking that he wrote without correction. However rapid might be his dispatch of prose composition, he thought long over his verse, and fashioned it with conscience and with care. After he had completed his translation of the first part of " Faust," he proceeded, with that amazing industry of the hand which is one of his remarkable characteristics, to copy it in exquisite caligraphy into a book. From this book he copied the whole once more for the printer, nor resting here, again reproduced it in his own hand for a gift of friendship.

The reiterated writing seemed to direct his attention to blemishes that otherwise lurked unseen. Writing was a great pleasure to him. " Do you know anything more fascinating than a great white virgin sheet of paper ? " he would sometimes ask. " Lars " and " The Prophet " and " Prince Deukalion " he copied into books which are now in the library of Harvard University. The poems that he brought back with him from the Orient, and which were published in 1854, he copied into a manuscript book which is now in the possession of Richard Henry Stoddard, and from it may be learned the date of the composition of each of the " Poems of the Orient." [1]

There is perpetual delight in these poems for him who loves a lyric line. They do not cloy with monotonous sweetness like Moore's Oriental idyls, nor weary with unpoetic diffuseness like Southey's never ending epics. They teach the eternal calm and brooding thought of the East. They relate stories that are full of dramatic force and fire, — " The Temptation of Hassan Ben Khaled," and " Amran's Wooing," are fascinating narratives deftly told. In one golden

[1] The dates of these poems will be found in the Appendix.

moment he minted the shining song whose immortality one feels to be secure. Beyond a doubt the magnificent " Bedouin Song " is a distinct addition to the imperishable things of our literature.

> " From the Desert I come to thee
> On a stallion shod with fire ;
> And the winds are left behind
> In the speed of my desire.
> Under thy window I stand,
> And the midnight hears my cry:
> I love thee, I love but thee,
> With a love that shall not die
>   *Till the sun grows cold,*
>   *And the stars are old,*
>   *And the leaves of the Judgment Book unfold !*

> " Look from thy window and see
> My passion and my pain ;
> I lie on the sands below,
> And I faint in thy disdain.
> Let the night winds touch thy brow
> With the heat of my burning sigh,
> And melt thee to hear the vow
> Of a love that shall not die
>   *Till the sun grows cold,*
>   *And the stars are old,*
>   *And the leaves of the Judgment Book unfold !*

> " My steps are nightly driven,
> By the fever in my breast,
> To hear from thy lattice breathed
> The word that shall give me rest.
> Open the door of thy heart,
> And open thy chamber door,

And my kisses shall teach thy lips
The love that shall fade no more
Till the sun grows cold,
And the stars are old,
And the leaves of the Judgment Book unfold! "

Taylor's "Orientalities" had what Moore, and Southey, and Monckton Milnes' "Palm-Leaves," and Victor Hugo's "Les Orientales" lacked, — a profound and vital appreciation of the life of the East. Ross Browne's Syrian dragoman, when he listened to the reading of "Hassan to his Mare," "sprang up with tears in his eyes, and protested that the Arabs talked just that way to their horses."

A poem, that is now printed among the "Poems of the Orient," but which was not written until May, 1869, entitled "Shekh Ahnaf's Letter from Baghdad," met with unfavorable comment as an improbable and unreal creation. It was declined by the "Atlantic Monthly," partly on account of its length, and partly because of its lack of dramatic truth. Yet here as always Taylor was sure of his subject, and was proceeding upon actual knowledge where his critics were walking in ignorance. He wrote to William D. Howells: "The letter is *genuine;* that is, such a letter describing just such a scene, *was* written from Bagdad by a Morocco Moslem; and I should not much wonder if the very things that might seem out of keeping with the character, to a reader, were the things which the Shekh *did* write. I found the letter a few weeks ago, and I altered nothing of his tone and manner, in the poem. Therein he seemed to me especially Moslem. This is a private explanation in my own justification; for I can easily see what must have appeared to you forced and undramatic. The letter made a deep impression upon me, so much so that I cannot dissociate it from the poem, and am therefore less able to judge objectively how it might strike another." [1]

Rich imagery and conscientious finish are the chiefest characteristics of these Oriental poems. The restraint or abstinence exerted by a writer so young and so ardent is more remarkable than the tropical opulence of Hugo or the magical melody of Rückert. " Daughter of Egypt, veil thine eyes ! " and " When Camadeva came " are models of artistic proportion and repression. The first challenges a comparison with anything of the same kind in literature. There are some Elizabethan and Caroline lyrics of release and delight that are finer in their way, but Taylor's song presents the moral nature recoiling upon the passionate and holding it in suppression.

[1] Written at Cedarcroft, May 10, 1869.

" Daughter of Egypt, veil thine eyes!
    I cannot bear their fire ;
Nor will I touch with sacrifice
    Those altars of Desire.
For they are flames that shun the day,
    And their unholy light
Is fed from natures gone astray
    In passion and in night.

" The stars of Beauty and of Sin,
    They burn amid the dark,
Like beacons that to ruin win
    The fascinated bark.
Then veil their glow, lest I forswear
    The hopes thou canst not crown,
And in the black waves of thy hair
    My struggling manhood drown ! "

" Camadeva " is the attempt to express the
most stupendous conception of the Hindu mythology, — the saturation or suffusion of the universe with the divinity of love.

" All breathing life a newer spirit quaffed,
    A second life, a bliss beyond a name,
And Death, half-conquered, dropped his idle shaft
    When Camadeva came."

Lowell feared that Bayard Taylor might become too deeply enamored of the sensuous in poetry, but when the wonder book that contained the best of Taylor's endeavor prior to his thirtieth year was closed, his style seemed to lose its fervor and intense expression. The scents and secrets of the East vanished, and

Taylor passed from the sensuous toward the psychological. In " L'Envoi " he bids —

> " Unto the Desert and the Desert steed
>   Farewell! The journey is completed now :
> Struck are the tents of Ishmael's wandering breed,
>   And I unwind the turban from my brow.

> " The sun has ceased to shine; the palms that bent,
>   Inebriate with light, have disappeared;
> And naught is left me of the Orient
>   But the tanned bosom and the unshorn beard."

He made a further collection of his poems, including a number of new ones, and published, in 1855, " Poems of Home and Travel." Then supervened a long period when but little poetry was written. He was fighting hard for freedom to live the life of which he dreamed and for which he planned. When Cedarcroft was acquired the poetical faculty reasserted itself. The great sorrow that had overshadowed his young life in the death of his first wife, and had driven him to foreign lands to ease the restless anguish of his heart, now found its voice in many poems that uttered the sad experience he had known. " Poets learn in sadness what they teach in song." Goethe said that he disposed of his griefs by putting them in a book. The memorable comparison of Thomas Moore reminds us that it is the wounded tree that drops the healing gum. " The Phantom,"

"Moan, ye wild winds around the pane!" and "She came, long absent from my side," are examples of the poems that commemorate the romantic attachment of Taylor's youth and its tragedy. When rest came, and his family was at home at Cedarcroft, he gathered the recollections of his moods, and told the story of his voyage from pain to peace, in "The Poet's Journal" (1862). He was vexed that the publishers should have advertised the book as the record of his life, for its associations were too sacred for the public square. He insisted that Ernest was but one half himself, and Edith only one fourth his wife, but the mischief had been done and the book that he should always most have prized became an almost painful memory. He had melted his sorrows and had run them into a mould from which he lifted a form of beauty that was a benefaction to the world. This was the spirit in which the work was performed : —

> "This arbor, too, was Ernest's hermitage :
>   Here he had read to me his tear-stained page
>   Of sorrow, here renewed the pang supreme
>   Which burned his youth to ashes ; here would try
>   To lay his burden in the hands of Song,
>   And make the Poet bear the Lover's wrong.
>   But still his heart impatiently would cry :
>   'In vain, in vain! You cannot teach to flow
>   In measured lines so measureless a woe,
>   First learn to slay this wild beast of despair,
>   Then from his harmless jaws your honey tear!'"

No part of " The Poet's Journal " is superior to the verses with which the book begins, inscribed "To the Mistress of Cedarcroft," — and closing : —

> " Come, for my task is done : the task that drew
> My footsteps from the chambers of the Day, —
> That held me back, Beloved, even from you,
> That are my daylight ; for the Poet's way
> Turns into many a lonely avenue
> Where none may follow.   He must sing his lay
> First to himself, then to the One most dear ;
> Last, to the World.   Come to my side, and hear !
>
> The poems ripened in a heart at rest,
> A life that first through you is free and strong,
> Take them and warm them in your partial breast,
> Before they try the common air of song !
> Fame won at home is of all fame the best ;
> Crown me your poet, and the critic's wrong
> Shall harmless strike when you in love have smiled,
> Wife of my heart, and mother of my child ! "

The entire poem is the glorification of family love, in its wholeness and its wholesomeness.

In June, 1850, he began to meditate a poem whose theme was pictorial art. He had then, he said, " no more serious purpose than to write a narrative poem of love and sorrow, with an artist as the hero." Either through a temporary failure of fancy, or a feeling of inadequacy to the task, he deferred completing the poem. Wherever he traveled the book went with him and grew with slow additions. In St. Peters-

burg, after the completion of " Hannah Thurston," he resumed the poem in earnest, and finished it in 1865, in the same year with " The
Story of Kennett," in a fury of composition,
" utterly absorbed, distrait, and lost for the material aspects of life." He named it " The Picture of St. John," and dedicated it to his artist
friends, Kensett, McEntee, Gifford, Church,
Colman, Whittredge, and Eastman Johnson.
Of all that company only Eastman Johnson and
F. E. Church are now alive. An early love
of color and form, and a certain skill in drawing, Taylor had never entirely neglected. From
his rambles abroad he brought home with him
sketches in oil and in water colors, of the landscapes and monuments that had impressed him.
In the Proem, " To the Artists," he wrote : —

> " Because the dream, thus cherished, gave my life
> Its first faint sense of beauty, and became
> Even when the growing years to other strife
> Led forth my feet, a shy, secluded flame :
> And ye received me, when our pathways met,
> As one long parted, but of kindred fate ;
> And in one heaven our kindred stars are set ;
> To you, my Brethren, this be dedicate ! "

Through the orderly and harmonic celebration of the artist's life that follows, runs the sustaining thought of the development of the artist's
power through his sympathy with the joy and
with the suffering of life. The latter is the

common theme of song everywhere in literature,
the former is the rarer and higher spirit that in-
spires " The Rime of the Ancient Mariner."

> " I loved my work; and therefore vowed to love
>   All subjects, finding Art in everything, —
>   The angel's plumage in the bird's plain wing, —
>   Until such time as I might rise above
>   The conquered matter, to the power supreme
>   Which takes, rejects, adorns, — a rightful king,
>   Whose hand completes the subtly-hinted scheme
>   And blends in equal truth the Fact and Dream ! "

After the first great sorrow of his life the Italian artist seeks a half forgetfulness in the cunning copying of Nature.   He paints

> " Each leaf and vein of meadow-blossoms pale,
>   The agate's streaks, the meal of mothy wings ! "

And when his soul is purged of the horrors
that possessed it, and his mind is cleansed of
" the unclean things that kept leets and law-days
there," he says : —

> " I wandered forth ; and lo ! the halcyon world
>   Of sleeping wave, and velvet-folded hill,
>   And stainless air and sunshine, lay so still !
>   No mote of vapor on the mountains curled ;
>   But lucid, gem-like, blissful, as if sin
>   Or more than gentlest grief had never been,
>   Each lovely thing, of tint that shone impearled,
>   As dwelt some dim beatitude therein !
>
>   .   .   .   .
>
> " So God's benignant hand directing wrought,
>   And Man and Nature took me back to life.
>   My cry was hushed : the forms of child and wife

Smiled from a solemn, moonlit land of thought,
A realm of peaceful sadness. Sad, yet strong,
My soul stood up, threw off its robes of strife,
And quired anew the world-old human song, —
Accepting patience and forgetting wrong ! "

The poem immediately gave Bayard Taylor an assured place among the poets of America. Longfellow called it " a great poem, — noble, sustained, and beautiful from beginning to end ; " Lowell decided that no American poem except " The Golden Legend " could match it in finish and sustained power ; and Joseph Knight, in the " Fortnightly Review " (March, 1867), passing upon the genius of Taylor, said, " He has not the earnestness of Longfellow, the wit of Lowell, or the breadth of Holmes, but in delicacy of workmanship and wealth of suggestion he transcends them all."

The stanza in which Taylor chose to cast this romantic epic of three thousand one hundred and seventy - six lines, was the *ottava rima*, treated as in the " Oberon " of Wieland. Hookham Frere in " The Monks and the Giants," Byron in " Don Juan," Moultrie in " Godiva," and the Etonians in general had, in their narrative verse, used the Italian stanza with the added spice of humor to relieve its uniform sweetness. Taylor secured a felicitous effect by capriciously varying the order of the rhymes in the stanza, introducing more than seventy variations, and so producing an arabesqueness of design that filled the poem with surprises. The unrestrained movement of the melody may be appreciated from the following stanzas : —

> " I found a girl before San Marco's shrine
> Kneeling in gilded gloom : her tawny hair
> Rippled across voluptuous shoulders bare,
> And something in the altar-taper's shine
> Sparkled like falling tears. This girl shall be
> My sorrowing Magdalen, as guilty-sweet,
> I said, as when, pure Christ ! she knelt to thee,
> And laid her blushing forehead on thy feet !

> " She sat before me. Like a sunny brook
> Poured the unbraided ripples softly round
> The balmy dells, but left one snowy mound
> Bare in its beauty : then I met her look, —
> The conquering gaze of those bold eyes, which made,
> Ah, God ! the unrepented sin more fair
> Than Magdalen kneeling with her humbled hair,
> Or Agatha beneath the quæstor's blade ! "

The chief defect of the poem is a certain immaturity of conception and juvenility of phrase. The "Proem," in which Taylor dubs his friends Opal, Bloodstone, Topaz, and Jacinth, is in precisely the vein which, in another, Taylor would have been the first to censure for affectation.

"The Picture of St. John" marks the close of the second stage of Bayard Taylor's development as a poet. He was soon absorbed in the study of Goethe, and his mind was taking on the cast of thought that was to determine his

future literary product, the first fruit of which
was "The Masque of the Gods" (1872). He
said of his studies at this time : "I read first of
all Goethe, then Montaigne, Burton, Mill, Buckle,
Matthew Arnold, and the old English poets ; of
the modern, chiefly Wordsworth, Tennyson, and
Clough. Ruskin and Carlyle serve as *entrées*.
I abhor everything spasmodic and sensational,
and aim at the purest, simplest, quietest style in
whatever I write. My ideal is as far off as ever,
but it has at least taken a clear, definite shape.
Instead of mist I see form. I have lost something of lyrical heat and passion, but gained in
feeling of proportion and construction." The
direction of his mind, as indicated by his reading, was evidently toward the religious and the
ethical. He was unusually familiar with the
Bible, and when the "Protestantenbibel" appeared, he studied it with keen interest. He
followed with close attention the researches of
Ebers and Lepsius in Egyptology, but found
little to sympathize with in Strauss, or in any
of the works of sheer negation. "I have been
reading," he writes to J. B. Phillips, March 23,
1871, "'Ecce Homo' and Darwin lately, and am
full of all sorts of prohibited doubts, for which
God be thanked ! — since doubt is always the
first step towards knowledge. Theological ruts
are the worst pitfalls under our feet."

Clearly the poems of his later years were to partake more of his searchings of the infinite, and his wrestlings with the problems of philosophy, than of the alert and light-hearted curiosity with which he had hitherto looked about him in the world, and blithely told his visions in lyric song. The loss of youthful freshness and delight was not to be compensated for by philosophical reflection; and the admixture of metaphysics effectually precipitated the poetry in " Prince Deukalion " and " The Prophet."

" The Masque of the Gods " was an inspiration. It was written at white heat in four days; and Taylor always regarded it as his best work. " Masque " seems an unfortunate word to describe a dramatic work so lofty in its intention, whose theme is the evolution of the human conception of the Deity. Three dialogues in the classical manner present, as Taylor defined the meaning of the book, " First, a colossal reflection of human powers and passions, mixed with the dread inspired by the unknown forces of nature; then, the idea of Law (Elohim), of Order and Beauty and Achievement (Jove and Apollo), and of the principles of Good and Evil (Persian), and of the Divine Love (Christ). But over all is the One supreme Spirit, yet unnamed, and whom men only now begin to conceive of, — the God of whom all previous gods gave only faint and various reflections, — to whom Christ is still nearest, but who was also felt, more or less dimly, in all creeds."

Christ, the revelation in man of the Divine Love, and Apollo, the representative of Art and Beauty, exist together in the poem, not in antagonism, but in harmony; indicating the corresponding nature of the beauty of holiness and the holiness of beauty.

> "One's face is fairer than the star of morning;
> One's voice is sweeter than the dew of Hermon
> To flowers that wither: who is there beside them?
> And is there need of any one above him
> Who brings his gifts of good and love and mercy?
> We climb to nobler knowledge, finer senses,
> And every triumph brings diviner promise,
> But Life is more: our souls for other waters
> Were sore athirst, till He unlocked the fountain.
> Now let us drink; for as a hart that panteth,
> Escaped from spears across the burning desert,
> We think to drain the brook, yet still it floweth."

The lyrical interludes and chorus of spirits are in the manner of Byron's "Manfred;" but Taylor's spirits talk better sense and poetry than Byron's, however inferior the dramatic environment of the "Masque" is to Byron's high imagination.

Longfellow was delighted with the work, and said to Taylor that he might now "safely write under it, *Fecit, fecit*, the double mark of Titian."

Taylor often composed a poem before he

wrote a line of it. His rapid dispatch of work therefore was misleading. Poems were held in suspension in his mi.. ~til ready to be transferred to paper. When he was meditating upon the " Centennial Ode," a difficult and responsible task, and some time before he actually began to write, he said, using a singular figure, " the string is in soak, and the thought is crystallizing upon it." With him the rule was first inspiration, then drudgery. The thought of " The Picture of St. John " he carried with him for fifteen years. " The Masque of the Gods," though written in four days, was long beforehand complete in his memory. Wordsworth and Tennyson sometimes lost poems that they had developed in thought : Taylor's memory never turned traitor. After the first draft he frequently rewrote his poems, often changing their metrical form. Several times he recast " Orso's Vendetta," " The Two Greetings," and " The Two Homes."

He never realized his conception more completely than in the idyllic narrative poem, " Lars : A Pastoral of Norway," which, although published in 1873, had been silently fixing itself to form for six years. It is historical that a community of Friends existed at Arendal in Norway : Quaker quiet by the shoulder of Berserk rage. Taylor's thought was to link the ancient pagan fury of the fells and fjords with the gentle speech and customs of the pastoral country of Pennsylvania. So the story begins and ends in Norway, but the intermediate events occur at Mt. Cuba, at the end of the Hockessin Valley, in the neighborhood of Kennett Square.

The poem is so severely simple, so perfectly proportioned, and so well within the author's powers, that it realized his ideal and won a place in critical esteem beside " Evangeline," and the best of Tennyson's corresponding verse. The simple Norway name " Lars " becomes the simple tale, though one learned Theban amended what he thought to be Taylor's faulty Latinity and made the title " Lares."

> " A herdsman, woodman, hunter, Lars was strong
> Yet silent from his life upon the hills.
> Beneath dark lashes gleamed his darker eyes
> Like mountain-tarns that take their changeless hue
> From shadows of the pine : in all his ways
> He showed that quiet of the upper world
> A breath can turn to tempest, and the force
> Of rooted firs that slowly split the stone.
> But Per was gay with laughter of the seas
> Which were his home."

And both these loved Brita, who was " glossy as a mating bird."

Their rivalry sets in bloody tragedy, and Lars leads exiled steps in foreign lands.

> " So Lars went onward, losing hope of good,
> To where, upon her hill, fair Wilmington

Looks to the river over marshy meads.
He saw the low brick church, with stunted tower,
The portal-arches ivied now and old,
And passed the gate : lo ! there, the ancient stones
Bore Norland names and dear, familiar words !

. . . .

" Led by a faith that rest could not be far,
Beyond the town, where deeper vales bring down
The winding brooks from Pennsylvanian hills,
He walked : the ordered farms were fair to see,
And fair the peaceful houses : old repose
Mellowed the lavish newness of the land,
And sober toil gave everywhere the right
To simple pleasures."

Again in this calm land, love for a pure and
gentle maiden, Ruth Mendenhall, springs up like
a fountain in him, and again the evil spirit in
his blood shrouds all his life in red anger, and
leads him to the edge of tragedy, when, with
murder in his heart and eye, he follows on fleet
foot his flying rival, Abner Cloud. And at the
last Lars wins peace and serenity of soul through
the love of Ruth, and on his native Norway soil
resists, like the Laird of Ury, the taunts and
challenges of the blood feud.

No poet ever returned with fonder recollection
to his humble birthplace, or sought with more
sincere devotion to lift its life and landscapes
into the clear air of art. In the best of his prose
works Taylor had made the name of Kennett
familiar to the readers of two continents. In six

pastorals and five ballads he interpreted the
spiritual meaning of the lives and scenery that
lay beyond the oaks and chestnuts of Cedarcroft.

The pastorals were written in hexameter verse.
which Taylor had studied in German literature
more than in English. His construction was
four feet dactylic, with occasional trochaic sub-
stitutions, the fifth foot inevitably a dactyl, the
line ending with a trochee or, now and then, a
spondee.

> "But since I am sated with visions,
> Sated with all the siren Past and its rhythmical phantoms,
> Here will I seek my songs in the quiet fields of my boyhood,
> Here where the peaceful tent of home is pitched for a season.
> High is the house and sunny the lawn : the capes of the wood-
>   lands,
> Bluff, and buttressed with many boughs, are gates to the dis-
>   tance
> Blue with hill over hill, that sink as the pausing of music.
> Here the hawthorn blossoms, the breeze is blithe in the or-
>   chards,
> Winds from the Chesapeake dull the sharper edge of the win-
>   ters,
> Letting the cypress live, and the mounded box, and the holly ;
> Here the chestnuts fall and the cheeks of peaches are crimson,
> Ivy clings to the wall and sheltered fattens the fig-tree,
> North and South are as one in the blended growth of the region,
> One in the temper of man, and ancient, inherited habits."

The sentiments of the slow, conservative farmers ; the "nasal monotonous chorals, sung by the
sad congregation ; " the stern sense of duty, that

> "Better it were to sleep with the owl, to house with the hornet,
> Than to conflict with the satisfied moral sense of the people,"

find their expression in these " pastorals " of one
who was cradled among the people, who knew
them and loved them. The peaceful farms, too,

> " The mossy roofs of the houses,
> Gables gray of the neighboring barns, and gleams of the high-
>   way
> Climbing the ridges beyond to dip in the dream of a forest,"

even the idle weeds that grow in the sustaining
corn, " the bitter-sweet, moon-seed, and riotous
fox-grape," are remembered, —

> " Flaring St. John's wort, milk-weed and coarse, unpoetical
>   mullein ; —
> Yet, were it not for the poets, say, is the asphodel fairer ?
> Were not the mullein as dear, had Theocritus sung it, or Bion ?
> Yea, but they did not ; and we, whose fancy's tenderest ten-
>   drils
> Shoot unsupported, and wither, for want of a Past we can
>   cling to,
> We, so starved in the Present, so weary of singing the Fu-
>   ture, —
> What is 't to us if, haply, a score of centuries later,
> Milk-weed inspires Patagonian tourists, and mulleins are
>   classic ? "

Not Whittier nor Barton nor any other of
the Friends has written a poem so dramatically
true and so replete with Quaker expressions as
Taylor's ballad, " The Quaker Widow," fore-
runner of " The Holly Tree," " John Reed,"
" Jane Reed," and " The Old Pennsylvania
Farmer."

" Home Pastorals, Ballads and Lyrics " (1875)

contains also some of Bayard Taylor's Odes. In his occasional poems made for public commemorations he essayed the Pindaric measure, never, save once, with popular success, but always with some degree of mechanical skill.

The "Gettysburg Ode," read at the dedication of the National Monument, July 1, 1869, as an imposed task cost him much trouble. He could not bend himself to poetry with the same prompt fluency with which he performed the prose tasks that were constantly set for him.

He took the text of the ode from Lincoln's address at Gettysburg.

> "From such a perfect text, shall song aspire
>   To light her faded fire,
>   And into wandering music turn
>   Its virtue, simple, sorrowful, and stern ?
>   His voice all elegies anticipated ;
>   For, whatsoe'er the strain,
>   We hear that one refrain :
> 'We consecrate ourselves to them, the Consecrated! ' "

Less successful was "Shakespeare's Statue," written for the unveiling of J. Q. A. Ward's statue of Shakespeare in Central Park (May 23, 1872). Another occasional poem was composed for the Goethe Club, to celebrate their presentation of a bust of Goethe to be placed in Central Park upon Goethe's one hundred and twenty-sixth birthday. Taylor's estimate of Goethe, his admiration of his " cosmical experience" and symmetrical culture, finds its amplest expression in the closing stanza : —

" Dear is the Minstrel, yet the Man is more ;
 But should I turn the pages of his brain,
 The lighter muscle of my verse would strain
And break beneath his lore.
 How charge with music powers so vast and free,
 Save one be great as he ?
Behold him, as ye jostle with the throng
Through narrow ways, that do your beings wrong,
 Self-chosen lanes, wherein ye press
 In louder Storm and Stress,
Passing the lesser bounty by
Because the greater seems too high,
 And that sublimest joy forego,
 To seek, aspire, and know !
Behold in him, since our strong line began,
The first full-statured man !
 Dear is the Minstrel, even to hearts of prose ;
But he who sets all aspiration free
Is dearer to humanity.
 Still through our age the shadowy Leader goes ;
Still whispers cheer, or waves his warning sign ;
 The man who, most of men,
Heeded the parable from lips divine,
 And made one talent ten ! "

General Hawley, the President of the United States Centennial Commission, invited Bayard Taylor to write the hymn for the opening day of the Exhibition, and asked him to name some one to compose the cantata. E. C. Stedman, who was the choice of the commission, had gone to Panama, and neither Theodore Thomas nor

Dudley Buck, the composer, would await his return. Taylor proposed the name of the Southern poet, Sidney Lanier, whose acquaintance he had made not many months before, and for the fine qualities of whose richly imaginative verse Taylor entertained the highest respect and admiration.

The commission had determined upon an oration and an ode for the great day when the centennial of the Declaration of Independence was to be celebrated. Hon. William M. Evarts was chosen to deliver the oration, but much difficulty was experienced in finding any one to accept the serious task of composing the ode. Longfellow and Lowell declined on the score of illness, Bryant because of age. Whittier and Holmes preferred that Taylor should make the attempt. When he assumed the new duty he withdrew his hymn, and so it happened that Bayard Taylor, representing Pennsylvania, produced the national ode, Georgia furnished the cantata, and Massachusetts sent the hymn from the pen of Whittier, who was by nature, as Taylor said, the high priest among American writers.

It is not often given to a poet to read his own verses to listening thousands and to kindle the public throng with the lofty aspirations of patriotism. The effect of Taylor's reading was electrical and wonderful. He was crowded upon by the spontaneous congratulation of the people, and his ears were dinned with the applause of the ten thousand who had heard and not heard the strains that, without manuscript or notes, he had repeated. He had elected to compose the ode in the Pindaric measure, and, in following that lofty precedent, to measure himself by the side of Lowell, and to invite comparison with the " Commemoration Ode." His work is nearly faultless from a technical point of view, in rhyme and cadence the lines flow on in smooth and harmonious succession ; but few of the verses cling, like Lowell's, to the memory, and with their high seriousness and grave melody kindle ennobling emotions of pride and patriotism.

Taylor's patriotism is exalted and inclusive. He is the most cosmopolitan of American authors.

> " He met the men of many a land,
> They gave their souls into his hand."

He was very comfortable in Germany, and he did not hesitate to acknowledge it ; he found much in America to reprove and to condemn, and he did not spare his censure. But never for an instant did he falter in his allegiance to his country, and his reverence for the invisible ideas upon which the progress of the nation is borne. In the Odes, he has done justice to patriotism, and in doing ample justice to the heroic type of character he has not breathed a syllable that could be construed into a glorification of war. Stopford Brooke has found fault with Tennyson for celebrating the brutalities of human struggle ; no later critic can discover the sentiment in Taylor.

Poetry was a veritable priestcraft with Bayard Taylor. It was his religion, and was to be approached only in serious mood. In his high conception art became a redemptive addition to human life. Although he was gifted with the acutest sense of humor, sometimes flashing into uproarious mirth, his conscientious consecration to poetry forbade the intrusion of it into his verse. He could no more disturb his verse with humor than the priest at the altar could pervert his sacred function. To the American humorist there is neither Jew nor Greek, neither bond nor free. Even Lowell is not free from sin in this particular. A jarring note grates on the reader of " The Cathedral " when its solemn thought is interrupted by an unnecessary comic digression.

For those who listened only to the tinkling cymbal Taylor frequently expressed his contempt, —

> " The dainty souls that crave
> Light stepping-stones across a shallow wave,
> Shrink from the deeps of Goethe's soundless song."

The only play of humorous verse that he per-mitted was the occasional indulgence of an un-usual genius for parody.   Like Talleyrand he found nonsense singularly refreshing.   Upon his Sunday evenings at home in New York he con-vulsed his guests with his volleys of puns and parodies.   At Fields' and at Graham's he set the table in a roar with his ridiculous improvisa-tions and his extraordinary quotations.   His was the famous etymology of restaurant, from *res*, a thing, and *taurus*, a bull: " a bully thing."   He demanded to know of a scholar who persisted in monopolizing the conversation with a disser-tation upon the sun myth, whether he knew the etymology of Smith ; and, setting scornfully aside the philological answer, asserted its deri-vation from " Sun-Myth " — Sumyth, Smyth, Smith.

His readiness was so remarkable that he could improvise for a whole evening in either English or German.   Professor W. T. Hewett, writing to me of Taylor's remarkable power of impro-visation, gives the following amusing illustra-tion : —

" I recall well an evening spent with him and a colleague at Mrs. P.'s (Pennock's).   Mr. Tay-lor was in fine spirits and full of droll sallies and humorous stories.   He turned to my colleague and said : 'F., do you remember that poem

which you wrote for one of the first numbers
of the Atlantic?'— *F.* 'No, I do not recall it
at the present time.' — *T.* 'I remember it very
well.' — *F.* 'Perhaps, as you remember it
better than I do, you will repeat it to the company.'— *T.* 'Certainly, with pleasure.' There-
upon Mr. Taylor began a long recital of the most
desperate rhymes, the most astounding plati-
tudes, and the most infamous verse which an
unanointed singer ever attempted. My clever
friend was without a retort. He had rashly chal-
lenged the production of what he knew did not
exist, but when Mr. Taylor's marvelous memory
had brought forth from its recesses an apparent
poem of his own, the product of his unleavened
youth, he was discomfited as I have never seen
him since. I believe that the company of young
people accepted absolutely my friend F. as the
author. I do not quote this as a specimen of
improvisation, but I have no doubt that impro-
visation entered into the marvelous product and
aided memory in numerous emergencies."

Years before Lewis Carroll had begun his exquisite imbecility of "portmanteau words," Taylor and Stoddard and O'Brien, in their midnight frolics with the eccentric muse, had
created verses that anticipated "The Lay of the
Jabberwock." Taylor cited as an example of
his own perverse imagination the lines:—

"Smitten by harsh transcetic thuds of shame
My squelgence fades : I mogrify my blame :
The lupkin world, that leaves me yole and blant,
Denies my affligance with looks askant."

When Edward Lear's "Book of Nonsense"
was young, verses of like character were made
by the New York triumvirate after they wearied
of parody. American literature in the latter
sixties showed tendencies with which Taylor
had no sympathy. Dialect verse he despised
and Western slang he abhorred. When dialect
abounded and vulgarity did much more abound,
American literature showed herself in some
sections a poor and ill-favored thing, — an
Audrey with raddled cheeks and kohl-smeared
eyes. Certain preposterous but popular poems
of farm life, in one of which the author makes
an American farmer say to his son, "Dowse the
glim!" excited the mirth of Taylor, who said :
"One can only laugh over such phenomenon ; it
does n't pay to be angry, and the public, if let
alone, will soon weary of its golden calves." [1]

Partly to prick the pretensions of some of the
portified posturers whose dervish tricks were
attracting attention ; partly to gratify his keen
sense of humor, and "to interpose a little ease"
in the busy race of toil, he composed burlesque

[1] Letter to J. B. Phillips, written at Kennett Square, September 11, 1871.

imitations of authors, living and dead, knit them together by the subterfuge of imaginary characters and a Broadway beer-cellar, and published the series under the title " The Echo Club and other Literary Diversions " (1872 and 1876).

It was not altogether parody, for there lurked amid the fun much suggestive history and criticism of our literature from the beginning of the nineteenth century, a subject which Taylor had it in his mind to write upon, but which circumstances prevented him from essaying.

When the papers of " The Echo Club " were written, we were entering in literature upon an era of nervous impatience and meretricious adornment. The bizarre and the superlative were the objects of literary quest. Taylor, who had been taught by Goethe, as Goethe had learned from Oesir, that simplicity is the ideal of beauty, admired quiet style and was parsimonious in epithet. His vexation at "the intense" prompted such a critical aside as the following : " I once discovered that with both the English and German poets of a hundred years ago evening is always called *brown* and morning either *rosy* or *purple*. Just now the fashion runs to jewelry ; we have ruby lips, and topaz light, and sapphire seas, and diamond air. Mrs. Browning even says : —

" ' Her cheek's pale opal burnt with a red and restless spark !'

What sort of a cheek must that be? Then we
have such a wealth of gorgeous color as never
was seen before, — no quiet half-tints, but pure
pigments, laid on with a palette-knife. Really, I
sometimes feel a distinct sense of fatigue at the
base of the optic nerve, after reading a magazine
story. The besetting sin of the popular — not
the best — authors is the intense."

"Angelo orders his Dinner" is the cleverest
of several clever parodies of Browning. An
"Ode on a Jar of Pickles" repeats Keats' "Ode
to a Nightingale." "Nauvoo" is a parallel of
Longfellow; but the original parody upon the
"Psalm of Life," which Bryant enjoyed and
which led Whitelaw Reid to suggest the making of a series of corresponding poems for the
"Tribune," Taylor declined to print lest there
should be offense in it. Swinburne and Emerson, Barry Cornwall and Rossetti, Bryant
and Tennyson, Mrs. Sigourney and Mrs. Browning, Boker and Read, Walt Whitman and Bret
Harte, and many more make up the ill-assorted
company of those whose literary secrets are dis-
sected in the light of day.

Taylor had at some time read "Nacoochee,
the Beautiful Star," "Virginalia," and "Eonchs
of Ruby," the crack-brained poems of Dr.
Thomas Holley Chivers of Georgia, whose imitations of Poe were the most grotesque of liter-

ary nightmares; and he retained in his memory the incongruous figures and extraordinary epithets of the poems. He had convulsed social companies with his quotations from them, and in the "Echo Club" he made Chivers the terrible example of a fashion in literature. Taylor's irresistibly comic manner lent additional force to such a stanza as the following from "Rosalie Lee:"—

> "Many mellow Cydonian suckets,
>   Sweet apples, anthosmial, divine,
> From the ruby-rimmed beryline buckets,
>   Star gemmed, lily shaped, hyaline;
> Like the sweet golden goblet found growing
>   On the wild emerald cucumber-tree,
> Rich, brilliant, like chrysoprase glowing,
>   Was my beautiful Rosalie Lee!"

There remains but one department of Bayard Taylor's poetic activity undescribed. Three times he essayed the drama. "The Masque of the Gods" has been noted; the others are "The Prophet," and "Prince Deukalion."

Thomas Bailey Aldrich at one time contemplated a dramatic poem to be called the "Seven Mormon Wives." He had about determined to abandon the project when he communicated it to Bayard Taylor. It curiously happened that at that time Taylor had already developed in his mind a similar plot to that proposed by Aldrich. In Gotha, in August, 1873, he began to write the play that had at intervals presented itself to him during a period of six years. At Friedrichrode, Weimar, and Leipzig, while occupied with his Goethe studies, he worked upon the drama, and finished it just one year after the completion of " Lars." It was called " The Prophet," and was published in 1874.

It is not a study in Mormonism, although its scene is laid among the Latter Day Saints, and their history is the background to the poem. The story instantly suggests Nauvoo, and the critics guessed the Prophet to be Joseph Smith. In David Starr, the protagonist of the play, there is no attribute of the Mormon leader. Starr is a fine idealist, not a vulgar sensualist. He is a victim of religious ecstasy, misled by false enthusiasm. When closely examined he is seen to be indicative of the spiritual direction, or the inner light, of the people of Taylor's own county. The actual prototype of the character, Taylor said, was the Rev. Edward Irving, although, apart from his belief in the bestowal of miraculous powers upon devout Christians, there is little to suggest the eloquent Scotch enthusiast, or his Holy Catholic Apostolic Church.

David Starr emigrates to the West, and establishes the community of Zion, intending to translate into practice the visions and raptures

of his life in New England. Polygamy is introduced into the plot, and the tragedy of the
Prophet's death concludes a story in which
unreasoning Orthodoxy is assailed at least as
roughly as Mormonism.

David Starr's vision in the wilderness is the
recollection of an actual experience that Taylor
had near the foothills of the Sierra Nevada in
1849. The Prophet says:—

> " Came languid peace, then awe and shuddering
>   Without a cause, a frost in every vein,
>   And the heart hammered, as to burst mine ears.
>   Something slid past me, cold and serpent like :
>   The trees were filled with whispers; and afar
>   Called voices not of man ; and then my soul
>   Went forth from me, and spread and grew aloft
>   Through darting lights, — His arrows, here and there
>   Shot down on earth.   But now my knowledge fades :
>   What followed, keener, mightier than a dream,
>   My hope interprets.   Only this I know, —
>   The dark invisible pillars of the sky
>   Breathed like deep organ-pipes of awful sound :
>   A myriad, myriad tongues the choral sang ;
>   And drowned in it, stunned with excess of power,
>   My soul sank down, and sleep my body touched."

The vision is the poetizing of a splendid
prose passage in " At Home and Abroad "
which recalls the strange dream-fugues of De
Quincey :—

" I lay awake half an hour at a time, watching the culmination of the stars on the meridian
line of a slender twig over my head. It was

perhaps an hour past midnight, when, as I thus lay with open eyes, gazing into the eternal beauty of the night, I became conscious of a deep, murmuring sound, like that of a rising wind. . . . A strange feeling of awe and expectancy took possession of me. Not a dead leaf stirred on the boughs ; while the mighty sound, — a solemn choral, sung by ten thousand voices, — swept down from the hills, and rolled away like retreating thunder over the plain. It was no longer the roar of the wind. As in the wandering prelude of an organ melody, note trod upon note, with slow majestic footsteps, until they gathered to a theme, and then came the words, simultaneously chanted by an immeasurable host : '*Vivant Terrestriœ!*' The air was filled with the tremendous sound, which seemed to sweep near the surface of the earth in powerful waves, without echo or reverberation."

It was Taylor's intention to publish " The Prophet " anonymously, and to prelude it with some verses by the unknown author, — the verses to be printed in " The Atlantic Monthly " or some other magazine. The plan was relinquished for various reasons, but the fact that such a design was entertained is interesting as illustrating the feeling that Taylor had for his poetry. At the time that he was engaged upon " The Prophet " he was much discouraged by the little attention paid to his poetical writings. His experience was precisely that of many literary men, who, after attaining a certain position, get scant praise from the newspapers. The good things of accredited authors are taken as matters of course, and poems and stories, any one of which would make the fortune of a new writer, create no enthusiasm whatever. On the eve of his departure for Cairo, and just after leaving Florence, — where, with Lowell and Henry James, he declared he had made "quite a Cambridge atmosphere in the very heart of the old Tuscan city," — he wrote to T. B. Aldrich : " As regards 'The Prophet' I think it can't make any serious difference. It *could not*, as I conceived it, be anything but a dramatic poem. A story would be very apt to betray me, and this will not. The manuscript will be copied and forwarded in April, and you can then judge. Meantime (as I have just written to Osgood) I 'll study ways and means of mystery, provocations of curiosity, etc., and forward whatever I can do in that line to you two, subject to your good judgment. I know *you* will like the work itself, for it is honest and earnest. When you suggested to me the *seven Mormon wives*, in the street, I had already my plan nearly complete, and it cost me an effort not to tell you so. I make the *origin* of the Mormon sect and the Joe Smith tragedy the historical background of my poem, but the plot has the universal human element. It stirs up more than one question which disturbs the undercurrents of the world, just nòw." (Rome, February 24, 1874.)

From Gotha, on his return from Egypt, Taylor wrote to Mr. Aldrich: "I have at last perpetrated three rather brief poems, which (to me) read as if they might have been written by some one else. The more I reflect upon the whole plan of mystification, the more difficult it seems to me. It is impossible to put forth 'The Prophet' as the work of a young poet, because no *young* poet could have written it: the mysterious author must be an older man, and some reason must be given — or indicated — why he has not before appeared in print." (May 21, 1874.)

The three poems were "A Lover's Test," "My Prologue," and "Gabriel," and they have been published in the "Household" edition of Taylor's poems. The reason why the unknown author has not before appeared in print, to which Taylor refers above in his letter to Mr. Aldrich, is hinted at in "My Prologue:" —

> "If heat of youth, 't is heat suppressed
> That fills my breast:
> The childhood of a voiceless lyre
> Preserv⋯ ⋯⋯

I chanted not while I was young ;
But ere age chill, I liberate my tongue !

" Apart from stormy ways of men,
    Maine's loneliest glen
Held me as banished, and unheard
    I saved my word :
I would not know the bitter taste
Of the crude fame which falls to them that haste.

" On each impatient year I tossed
    A holocaust
Of effort, ashes ere it burned,
    And justly spurned.
If now I own maturer days,
I know not : dust to me is passing praise.

" But out of life arises song,
    Clear, vital, strong, —
The speech men pray for when they pine,
    The speech divine
No other can interpret : grand
And permanent, for time and race and land.

" I dreamed I spake it : do I dream
    The pride supreme,
Or, like late lovers, found the bride
    Their youth denied,
Is this my stinted passion's flow ?
It well may be ; and they that read will know."

The poems are so Taylorian in every respect
that even had they been published as intended,
their authorship could not have been the mystery of an hour.

The ethical thought of " The Masque of the

Gods" matured and culminated in "Prince Deukalion," Bayard Taylor's last play and last book. His religious faith which had swung so wide from its early moorings was definitely defined in this last testament. It was the audit of his personal account : his conception of life and of the universe. The great idea of immortality that has held men through all the ages, and has been the centre of so much of the world's grandest literature, is the central fire burning in this rhyme of the progress of humanity.

Early in life Taylor had a dream, the effect of which was never lost. He dreamed that he had been shot. The wound was mortal, and the extrication of the soul from the body and its subsequent independent life were so vivid as to be accepted as a revelation. The strange vision gave him an inexpugnable sense of personal immortality. Before going to Germany for the last time, Taylor showed to the Rev. W. R. Alger a drawing of the dead Goethe, and remarking the sweetness of contentment that rested upon the features, said that it was the signet of immortality left by the departing tenant upon the mortal clay.

Immortality was to him a profound and undisturbed conviction, and he bore witness to it when all about him materialism was shaking to destruction the established dogmas of the world.

He read little in metaphysics, but he meditated much upon Goethe's " Pandora " and upon the second part of " Faust." He was in the habit of introspectively taking and giving account of himself. When he believed himself to have arrived at a final *Weltanschauung*, to use a German word which he might have used and for which there is no exact equivalent in English, he attempted to give it literary expression, believing with Dr. Hedge that even metaphysics might be sung if first melted in the poetic mood ; hence in " Prince Deukalion " the grasping at the whole of human history, and the projection of the poet's imagination into the time to come. The symbolism of the drama has condemned it to be read by a very few, but popularity is no test of real merit. The barest commonplace, if enveloping a sentiment that touches the common heart of man, is treasured up to a life beyond life, while the great reaches of thought and imagination are shared and transmitted by an elect few of mankind. Sydney Smith, when he delivered his lectures on moral philosophy at the Royal Institution, began with : " There is a word of dire sound and horrible import which I would fain have kept concealed if I possibly could. It is that very tremendous one of METAPHYSICS, which in a lecture on Moral Philosophy seems likely to produce as much alarm as the cry of fire in a crowded play-house, when Belvidera is left to weep by herself and every one saves himself in the best manner he can." Probably not many of those who essayed "Prince Deukalion" held on to the close of the first act, and of those who read further there was likely but a handful who found the Roman Catholic Church in the symbolism of the Medusa, or who in the fourth act realized the scope of Taylor's hope and imagination for the future and the giant things to come at large.

From savagery to refined civility, from the stone age to the golden age, the long and devious journey of humanity is recorded in this lyrical drama. To Buddha preaching the gospel of renunciation, Agathon replies, expressing Taylor's whole philosophy of life : —

> " But I *accept*, — even all this conscious life
> Gives in its fullest measure, — gladness, health,
> Clean appetite, and wholeness of my claim
> To knowledge, beauty, aspiration, power !
> Joy follows action, here ; and action bliss,
> Hereafter !   While, God-lulled, thy children sleep,
> Mine, God-aroused, shall wake to wander on
> Through spheres thy slumbrous essence never dreamed.
> Thy highest is my lowest ! "

The metrical variety of the work makes it one of the notable poems of America. The structural five stress verse undulates into light and sparkle. The lyrical interludes and choral passages shift into protean shapes, and the reminiscences of German and English literature lend a faint perfume even to lines that otherwise are dull or languid.

A melancholy interest attaches to " Prince Deukalion." The manuscript book was completed October 7, 1877. In November of the following year it was published. Only one copy of the work did Bayard Taylor see. It was his " swan-song." Within a month he was dead.

In gathering up all the strands of Bayard Taylor's poetic genius, — lyric, epic, ode, idyl, romance, pastoral, and drama, — and knitting them into one brave pattern, that by their united lustre his work as a whole may be accounted for, and his place in literature determined, it is immediately evident that his character adequately and justly expressed itself in his poetry. His buoyancy of spirit, his gentle disposition, his stainless morals, and his loyalty to the best in himself and in his friends, in a word all the predominating traits of his life, are also the chief accents of his verse.

Whittier " so loved the man ; " Longfellow compared him to his own ideal Prince, —

> " Thou hast sung with organ tone
> In Deukalion's life thine own ; "

Powers spoke of him as almost an angel ; " in soul and stature larger than thy kind," said

Lanier. The manly and magnanimous nature that stole away the hearts of men and made them his, informed his poetry, into which no discordant note of envy or of malice enters. His worst he kept, his best he gave.

He has sensuous passion, but it is clean and pure. He stretches wide arms to grasp the joy of earth, but he always holds himself in a restraining grasp. Upon new acquaintances he made an impression of innocence. His conduct and his conversation did not betray the wide knowledge of men and of the world that he really possessed. He took literature seriously and his life was simple. He was neither a churchman, nor a man of the world; he was consecrated to poetry, and he was a member of the universal church invisible.

He began his career singing his simple delight in the kindly earth, with Bryant for the master of his youth. The elemental feeling that he caught from his master is illustrated in "The Bath," a poem that might have been written by Walt Whitman, could he by some strange miracle have been converted to art. "Run Wild" illustrates with equal force Taylor's feeling for natural scenery.

He outgrew the "elemental" and the lyrical, and entered upon the ethnical and secular. Historic and prophetic visions, the infinite cavalcade of nations and races, and the procession of the ages, superseded the "desert's utmost rim," and the "land of Dreams and Sleep." An alert perception of external things was in his verse as in his prose. A fine sense of form and color distinguished the oriental images and "The Picture of St. John." He was far from affectation. "Proportion" was his word for art. His instinct was against obscurity and odd expression, — an admirable and enviable instinct in these days when, as George Eliot has said, "Clear messages are rare," and when a Browning gives us, as it were, Anglo-Saxon drawings, when he might as easily render his subject in correct anatomy.

Taylor has splendid rhetoric. His verse is strikingly sonorous, and he was always seeking what he called "resonance." There is a roll to some of the lines of his "Faust" that suggests a far-sounding march. He was fond of broad, bright vowels and rich consonantal effects, and was skillful in the disposition of them. His alliteration was voluminous yet subtle. The opening of "The National Ode" is full of these qualities.

> " Sun of the stately Day,
>   Let Asia into the shadow drift,
>   Let Europe bask in thy ripened ray,
>   And over the severing ocean lift

> A brow of broader splendor!
>   Give light to the eager eyes
> Of the Land that waits to behold thee rise;
>   The gladness of morning lend her,
>   With the triumph of noon attend her,
> And the peace of the vesper skies! "

The glittering march of the stanzas of " The Lost Crown," —

> " A throne of gold the wheels uphold,
>   Each spoke a ray of jeweled fire:
> The crimson banners float unrolled
>   Or falter when the winds expire," —

and the lofty diction of " Canopus," —

> " And, past those halls which for itself the mind
>   Builds, permanent as marble, and as cold,
> In warm surprises of the blood we find
>   The sumptuous dream unfold! " —

display a mastery of rhetoric and harmony unsurpassed in American poetry.

He was accompanied by the melodies of other poets. They haunted him, and so shaped his own work that they conveyed to the critical ear familiar sounds and created the impression that Taylor was only a copier of others. Yet he was always trying metrical experiments, and he was proud of his sure-footed verse. His poem " The Waves " (1850), conceived while walking on the Battery in New York, was an attempt to suggest " the rapid rolling to shore of the waves under a fresh breeze."

In " Wind and Sea " a striking effect is produced by the opposition of the two elements in movement. These poems and " Iris " show how Taylor was charged with Shelley, an influence that yielded later to the spirit of Tennyson, who is felt in the delicate fancy of the improvisation : —

> "A grass-blade is my warlike lance,
>   A rose-leaf is my shield ;
> Beams of the sun are, every one,
>   My chargers for the field.
>
> " The morning gives me golden steeds,
>   The moon gives silver-white ;
> The stars drop down, my helm to crown,
>   When I go forth to fight.
>
> " Against me ride in iron mail
>   The squadrons of the foe :
> The bucklers flash, the maces crash,
>   The haughty trumpets blow.
>
> " One touch, and all, with armor cleft,
>   Before me turn and yield.
> Straight on I ride ; the world is wide,
>   A rose-leaf is my shield !
>
> " Then dances o'er the waterfall
>   The rainbow, in its glee ;
> The daisy sings, the lily rings
>   Her bells of victory.
>
> " So am I armed where'er I go,
>   And mounted night or day :
> Who shall oppose the conquering rose,
>   And who the sunbeam slay ? "

An English critic says that " the main draw-back to the widespread acceptance of Bayard Taylor's poetry as a whole is its perpetual dif-fuseness. His most ambitious productions are marred by a ceaseless effort to overstrain his powers." There is a truth in this acute though curt criticism that was the keenest disappoint-ment of Taylor's life. Exhausting and multi-form labors perpetually forbade him to refine his subtle sense of poetry, and to overtake the splendid ideal that he pursued. The permanent works of the human spirit seem to require soli-tude and repose for their creation. The great German declares,

> " Es bildet ein Talent sich in der Stille,
> Doch ein Charakter in dem Strom der Welt."

In his eager quest after " cosmical experi-ence," and in his hungry ambition " to dwell enlarged in alien modes of thought," Taylor lost the opportunity and ability to overtake the one thing that he really reverenced and for which he lived. " If I were to write about myself for six hours," he wrote to E. C. Stedman, " it would all come to this : that life is, for me, the establish-ing of my own *Entelecheia*, — the making of all that is possible out of such powers as I may have, without violently forcing or distorting them."

Fierce competition and a life of hurry were the conditions under which Taylor labored.

He had a generous scheme of living, and he had a severely high ideal ; with splendid health and courage he struggled to win the one, and to realize the other. The swiftest runner could hardly hope to win in such a race. Taylor sank exhausted when almost at the goal. When with failing breath he panted, "I want that stuff of life"— almost the last words that passed his lips, — it was the pathetic, even tragic, cry of a strong man whose work still lay before him, and upon whose dying brow the light of an ideal that could never be attained still lingered. When under the German spell, and when his spiritual nature was spongy to the imagination and melody of Goethe and Schiller, his verse led on into richer and more various measures that indicated what might have been, had the tyranny of his surroundings been more merciful, and had time been vouchsafed him for the successful and solitary pursuit of his serene ideal.

His emancipation from the "cabin'd, cribb'd, confined" life in Pennsylvania, and later from the retarding influences of an insufficient society in New York, was slow and uncertain. The men of New England were content with plain homes and simple living, and were satisfied with the small incomes of professional life. Taylor had other aims. He was ambitious for himself and thoughtful for his friends. Involved in the expenses of Cedarcroft he never knew the enormous value of freedom. He was always drawing on the strength of to-morrow to do the work of to-day; as machinists say, he was running on his gudgeons. Where so much was done, and work was so profuse and so constant, it is still a matter of surprise that the average was so fine. Uhland says : —

> "Fehlt das äussre frie Wesen
> Leicht erkrankt auch das Gedicht." [1]

And unconsciously Taylor was, in himself, a fresh illustration of the truth of the saying. His failure was more admirable than many successes. "Not failure but low aim is crime," says Robert Browning, who preaches the gospel of lofty endeavor in "Rabbi Ben Ezra," "The Grammarian's Funeral," and a score of other poems. Taylor's ambition could scarcely have been fully realized even in a long life strictly dedicated, as Prospero on the enchanted island says, "to closeness, and the bettering of his mind with that which but by being so retired, o'erprized all popular rate." Amid his many distractions, and under his weary load, it was impossible.

The discontent and the longing are in "Implora Pace : " —

[1] *Vorwort*, 1st edition, 1815.

" And still some cheaper service claims
    The will that leaps to loftier call :
Some cloud is cast on splendid aims,
    On power achieved some common thrall.

" To spoil each beckoning victory,
    A thousand pygmy hands are thrust ;
And, round each height attained, we see
    Our ether dim with lower dust.

" Ah, could we breathe some peaceful air,
    And all save purpose there forget,
Till eager courage learn to bear
    The gadfly's sting, the pebble's fret !

" Let higher goal and harsher way,
    To test our virtue, then combine !
'T is not for idle ease we pray,
    But freedom for our task divine."

No one ever felt more intensely than Bayard
Taylor " the torment and the ecstasy " of verse.
His friend, Richard Henry Stoddard, says :
" Taylor's nature was so ardent, so full-blooded,
that slight and common sensations intoxicated
him, and he estimated their effect, and his power
to transmit it to others, beyond the true value."
The poetic temperament sees the beauty of the
world as the unanointed eye cannot. The radiance in flood and field, the transfiguring light
upon the landscape Taylor thought he had completely captured, in words which to him were a
wilderness of blooms and scents, but which were
commonplace to other eyes.

There are several poems in which he celebrates his own genius, and the glory of his poetic effort and achievement. It is not egotism that prompts such creations as " Porphyrogenitus," and " The Lost Crown." In them he speaks for men of his type, and through them to universal humanity. In all his literary work he availed himself of his experience and of his moods. His soul in the poetic celebrations of himself takes reflex possession of its own glory.

Taylor's chief defect seems to me to be a lack of spontaneity. His poetry is all *intended*. It is carefully built up by the intellect. The reader searches in vain for an escape from the intellectual ; Taylor never gives the rein to the spirit. The reader is surprised by no sudden glories of imagination, for Taylor never seems to look forth from those " magic casements, opening on the foam of perilous seas in faery lands forlorn ! "

In the " Bedouin Song," in " The Song of the Camp," with its athletic stanzas, —

> " They lay along the battery's side,
> Below the smoking cannon :
> Brave hearts from Severn and from Clyde,
> And from the banks of Shannon," —

and in the exquisite melody and tender pathos of " Euphorion," Bayard Taylor rises very near the heaven of highest song. Of the longer, sustained poems, " Lars " only seems to contain the principle of life.

A Taylor cult exists in America. Among the younger poets his verse is carefully studied. Clubs exist in schools and colleges, at least in New York and Pennsylvania, for the reading of his works. Charles Henry Lüders in " The Dead Nymph," and Frank Dempster Sherman in a " Greeting for Spring," [1] have essayed the style of " Peach-Blossom," and in many another poem have followed the music of Taylor. Clinton Scollard, who has been an enthusiastic collector and interpreter of Taylor's poetry, has been inspired by its lyrical spirit to the making of some of his strongest and most vital verse.

Three months before his death, Bayard Taylor wrote his last poem, " Epicedium. William Cullen Bryant." He was desperately ill and exhausted, and he knew that the verses were sluggish and forced. The closing lines, the last that Taylor ever penned, are as true of their author as of Bryant.

> " His last word, as his first, was Liberty!
> His last word, as his first, for Truth
> Struck to the heart of age and youth:
>   He sought her everywhere,
> In the loud city, forest, sea, and air:
> He bowed to wisdom other than his own,
>   To wisdom and to law,
>   Concealed or dimly shown
> In all he knew not, all he knew and saw,
> Trusting the Present, tolerant of the Past,

[1] Published in *Lyrics for a Lute.*

> Firm-faithed in what shall come
> When the vain noises of these days are dumb;
> And his first word was noble as his last!"

On the road from Gotha to Friedrichroda is a stork's nest upon the gable of a peasant's house in the little village of Wahlwinkel. After one of the drives from Gotha, Bayard Taylor wrote "The Village Stork," a poem which is the immediate precursor of "Epicedium." Reading between the lines it is not difficult to catch an undertone of sadness and personal meaning. It contains his wanderings, his long struggle for recognition and opportunity, and his still uncertain place in poetry.

The Stork is made to say: —

> "Beneath a sky forever fair,
>   And with a summer sod,
> The land I come from smiles — and there
>   My brother was a god!
> My nest upon a temple stands
>   And sees the shine of desert lands;
> And the palm and the tamarisk cool my wings,
> When the blazing beam of the noonday stings,
>   And I drink from the holy river!

> "There I am sacred, even as here;
>   Yet dare I not be lost,
> When meads are bright, hearts full of cheer,
>   At blithesome Pentecost.
> Then from mine obelisk I depart,
>   And sweep in a line over Libyan sands
>   To the blossoming olives of Grecian lands,
> And rest on the Cretan Ida!

" Parnassus sees me as I sail ;
    I cross the Adrian brine ;
The distant summits fade and fail,
    Dalmatian, Apennine ;
The Alpine snows beneath me gleam,
I see the yellow Danube stream ;
    But I hasten on till my spent wings fall
    Where I bring a blessing to each and all,
And babes to the wives of Wahlwinkel !

" She drooped her head and spake no more ;
    The birds on either hand
Sang louder, lustier than before, —
    They could not understand.
Thus mused the stork, with snap of beak :
' Better be silent, than so speak !
    Highest being can never be taught !
    They have their voices, I my thought ;
And they were never in Egypt ! ' "

When the extraordinary range of his interests
and efforts is considered, and his variety and
cosmopolitanism weighed, it appears that other
poets of America have surpassed him in parts
but that no one has equaled him in all. Longfellow has culture and goodness, Taylor has
also passion ; Whittier is ethical, Taylor is also
philosophical. Emerson has more of mystic
originality, greater *élan* of inspiration, and ex-
cels in transcendental audacity ; Longfellow
preserves a more equal flight and has greater
average fittedness to popular appreciation ; Lowell surpasses him in scholastic refinement, and
wit, and satire, and in height of imagination.

Bayard Taylor's themes are noble; his material deep, rich, and weighty; his diction flexible, precise, concise, and musical; and his poetic form filed and finished in the spirit of artistic unity.

CHAPTER VII.

LAST DAYS AND DEATH.

1874–1878.

JAMES RUSSELL LOWELL says of Masson's vast life of John Milton that Milton occasionally enters the biography, and, like Paul Pry, hopes he does not intrude. The merry comparison would not hold in Bayard Taylor's relations to American literature. Consider the work he did in the fifty-four years of his life : his far travels, his wide experience in all departments of journalism, his services as a diplomatist in Russia and in Germany, the variety of his literature, — essays, descriptive and critical, history and biography, novels and short stories, translations, odes, idyls, ballads, lyrics, pastorals, dramatic romances, and lyrical dramas, — and it is clear that his career comprehends the orbit of contemporary American life and letters. He was not our highest and most influential writer ; he was rather a *meister-singer*, — a guild-singer, — a man of talent, and master of the mechanics of his craft. But on all sides he

touched the life of his time.   He was one of the
most widely known American authors.   Art had
graven him in romantic garb upon the public
mind.   Astonishing memory and prodigious industry in him had taken the place of genius, and
they had won a signal triumph.

After his return to America in September,
1874, work crowded upon him.   He had become
a noted man ; the public exacted services from
him ; his correspondence became enormous and
he neglected none of it, writing scores of letters
in a day.   He found a great demand for his
lectures, and he accepted all engagements in
order to rid himself of debt and to obtain freedom to pursue the biography of Goethe and
Schiller.   In the first six months after landing
he lectured one hundred and thirty times, and
traveled fifteen thousand miles.   Eleven thousand dollars he cleared by this labor, and so
made himself easy for a year to come.   At the
same time he repeated his lectures at Cornell
University, described the Bunker Hill Centennial for the " Tribune," and revised his translation of " Faust " for the " Kennett edition,"
which was published in the autumn of 1875.
The summer he spent at Mattapoisett upon Buz-
zard's Bay, sketching, and writing " Alongshore " letters to the " Tribune."   " Ion of
Iceland " appeared in " St. Nicholas," and many

book reviews were furnished to the " Tribune "
and the " International Review." When the
year closed he was living in comfortable quarters in New York, in the Stuyvesant Building,
142 East Eighteenth Street. He was unutter-
ably weary of being bumped about the country
in railway trains, sleeping in shabby hotels, and
racking his voice in draughty halls, where the
wild winds flew round sobbing in their dismay.
Any employment seemed preferable to a con-
tinuance of lecturing. He resolved to go back
to his newspaper desk, and bend his head beneath the midnight gas. He agreed to edit
" Picturesque Europe " for the Appletons, and
entered upon daily work in the " Tribune "
office. He did not spare himself. For twenty
years he had been free from the newspaper
routine ; now he trod it patiently and conscien-
tiously, though at his age and with his reputation he should have been rid of it entirely.

During 1876 he carried forward this new
burden of affairs. George Ripley was head of
the literary department of the " Tribune," and
under him Taylor prepared book reviews, and
wrote such leading articles as " *In re* Walt
Whitman," " Authorship in America," " George
Sand," and " Antonelli." The leaders upon
European politics in the majority of cases were
written by him, and a large amount of miscella-

neous work was also done.   To show how cruelly
he overworked himself I have counted his contributions to the " Tribune " and find that in 1876
he gave that paper two hundred and thirteen
articles of every description, — letters, reviews,
and editorials.   In 1877 he printed one hundred
and eighty-five articles, and in the first seven
weeks of 1878 thirty-three more appeared.

He occasionally lectured, and he delivered
his Cornell lectures before the Peabody Institute
in Baltimore.   The " Centennial Ode " was
written and read, and his last prose work was
published.   It was a children's classic : " Boys
of Other Countries, Stories for American Boys."

He began, at the suggestion of Mr. Whitelaw
Reid, a series of papers upon " Life and Habits
Abroad," which, when completed in the " Weekly
Tribune," would have made another volume.
But two of these articles appeared : " Ways
of Living in Italy " (" Tribune," January 12,
1878), which shows Taylor's minute observation
and prodigious memory, — he even notes the
fact that in Italy " a small farmer," or one who
farms seven or eight acres, will use, with his
family, two barrels of oil, and eight barrels of
wine in a year, — and " Common Life in Spain "
(" Tribune," February 13, 1878).

His hands were full of tasks.   He was cut to
the heart that his poetry, and the " Life of

Goethe " — his darling project — had to be postponed. Hurried and fagged as he was, his health
began to fail. He lost the alacrity of mind and
cheer of manner that had characterized him.
He no longer took delight in social recreation,
but became grave and abstracted. As his vitality
waned, his absent-mindedness increased. Un-
like his old intense self, he seemed not to hear
things that were said to him, although he answered mechanically.

He writes to Sidney Lanier (March 12, 1877):
" Drudgery, drudgery, drudgery! What else
can I say? Does not that explain all? Two
courses of twelve lectures on German Literature, here and in Brooklyn, daily work on the
' Tribune,' magazine articles (one dismally de-
layed), interruptions of all sorts, and just as
much conscience as you may imagine pressing
upon me to write to you and other friends!
The fact is I am so weary, fagged, with sore
spots under the collar-bone, and all sorts of
indescribable symptoms which betoken lessened
vitality, that I must piteously beg you to grant
me much allowance."

Again he writes to Lanier: " I am ground to
the dust with work and worry. I live from day
to day, on the verge of physical prostration.
Nothing saves me but eight to ten hours of death-
like sleep, every night. Of course everything

must wait, — my Life of Goethe, my lyrical drama, everything that is solely and dearly mine."

In 1877 a few additional lecture tours were undertaken, and he exposed himself to hardship and fatigue. The work of art criticism was added to his other "Tribune" duties; he repeated his lectures at Cornell University, and spent some restful days with Professor Willard Fiske. In June, he wrote "Soldiers of Peace," a poem for the Grand Army of the Potomac, a task which in the previous year he had transferred to William Winter. The month of July he spent at White Sulphur Springs in the hope of recovering from the dropsical symptoms that were appearing. The remainder of the summer at Newport and Mattapoisett so far "wound up the slackenëd strings of his lute " that, with the return of the poetic faculty, he resumed work upon "Prince Deukalion," and completed it on the third of October, when he immediately took up Schiller's "Don Carlos" with the intention of translating and adapting it for Lawrence Barrett. His letters to the "Cincinnati Commercial " were continued, frequent articles were contributed to the magazines, and his Cornell lectures were re-delivered at the Lowell Institute.

It was rumored in 1877 that Bayard Taylor was to be appointed to a foreign mission. The

hope of completing the double biography of
Goethe and Schiller made Taylor wish that he
might be fortunate enough to secure the German
ministry. He was too poor to accept an appointment to any other foreign court. Berlin
he knew well enough to know that he could live
there upon his salary; and then the splendid
opportunity for literary and scholastic work!
Private collections and public archives that
would otherwise be inaccessible would open to
him as ambassador.

After his return to Kennett Square from the
Springs in Virginia, he wrote (August 7, 1877)
to Professor J. Morgan Hart : " My biography
of Goethe is my sole absorbing interest, and *that
alone* impels me, now, to await the pleasure of
the government, which may either give or take
away my chance of completing the great design
within the next two or three years. . . . I cling
to my plan with such tenacity that I surely must
be allowed to accomplish it before I die."

The government moved slowly in its appointments. Taylor made no personal application,
and in conversation with the President made
no reference to the rumors flying through the
press. At last, on the fifteenth of February,
1878, President Hayes sent Bayard Taylor's
name to the Senate as Minister to Germany.
Among the many admirable appointments made

by the President none was more creditable to him or more acceptable to the country. Taylor made no effort to conceal his supreme delight. At last his time had come. With some leisure, with much prestige, the way was open for him to the realization of his cherished hopes. From all sections of the country poured in congratulations and good wishes. " I felt as if buried under a huge warm wave of congratulation," he wrote to Lanier.

A letter to William D. Howells expresses his delight, and his hope for the future.

142 EAST 18TH ST., NEW YORK, *February* 20, 1878.

MY DEAR HOWELLS, — My wife joins her thanks to mine for your kind congratulation, which came just between Whittier's " God bless thee ! " and a lusty shout from Whipple. You may guess from what I said under your roof, that the appointment was a great surprise ; but a greater surprise and a better honor came to me in the universal generosity of the response to it. Of course I am glad, — for now nothing stands between me and the life of Goethe.

Ever faithfully yours,

BAYARD TAYLOR.

Until April 11, when he sailed, Taylor was the pet of the people ; receptions and dinners

filled the period. He was amazed and over-
whelmed. The Union League of Philadelphia,
the Goethe Club of New York, the German
Minister in Washington, the Deutsche Gesellig-
Wissenschaftliche Verein of New York entertained him. The two demonstrations that were
most precious to him were in West Chester and
at the Century Club. The banquet at the former place is still a famous memory in Chester
County. At the latter the most eminent men
of the country pressed upon him with spontaneous recognition and congratulation. George
William Curtis in an Easy-Chair paper writes
of the latter demonstration : " The good-fellow-
ship of the Century is famous and traditional,
and the breakfast to Mr. Taylor assembled some
sixty Centurions, with Mr. Bryant at their
head, to congratulate Brother Bayard on the
honors which had naturally fallen upon an associate. There were, besides Mr. Bryant, three or
four of the original members, the patriarchs, the
fathers, the founders of the Century, who had
been members of the old Sketch Club, from
which it grew, and whose presence gives the
Century the true royal flavor, like the lump
of ambergris in the Sultan's cup."

Champagne, and flowers, and smiles, and
blessings followed him to the pier at Jersey
City. A tug bearing the German flag accom-

panied the Holsatia down the bay.   When the
last bottle had been opened, and the last farewells had been spoken, and the vessel stood forth
to sea, Bayard Taylor, exhausted and overcome,
sought his stateroom.

Mr. William D. Howells, in his account of
his first visit to New England, has described
"the tremendous adieux" which were paid Bayard Taylor in New York: "Some of us who
were near of friendship went down to see him
off when he sailed, as the dismal and futile
wont of friends is ; and I recall the kind, great
fellow standing in the cabin, amid those funereal
flowers that heaped the tables, saying good-by
to one after another, and smiling fondly, smiling wearily, upon all.   There was champagne,
of course, and an odious hilarity without meaning and without remission, till the warning bell
chased us ashore, and our brave poet escaped
with what was left of his life."   ("Harper's
Magazine," May, 1894.)

Three days of opiates quieted the dangerous
excitement that had brought on insomnia and
had threatened brain fever ; then the ocean seda-
tive calmed the fierce blood.   In England he met
Max Müller and Thomas Carlyle.   He went to
Paris to be present at the opening of the Exposition.   There he had "a queer midnight supper"
with Victor Hugo, and attended MacMahon's
grand reception at his palace.

His reception in Germany was sincerely cordial. The Crown Prince waived the customary formalities of presentation, saying that Bayard Taylor needed no introduction in Germany. With Bismarck he had two interesting interviews. In one day he saw and conversed with Bismarck, Gortchakoff, Beaconsfield, Andrassy, Waddington, Mehemet Ali Pasha, Curtius, Mommsen, Lepsius, and Helmholtz. The business of the embassy called for close attention and nice management. The cases of naturalized German citizens who had returned to Germany and fallen into difficulties caused him considerable trouble. He wrote to the Department of State, " The experience of the legation includes so many instances of ignorant and overweening assumption of rights, that a certain amount of indiscretion, to use no stronger term, may be reasonably inferred in at least half the cases where an appeal is made for official intervention." (August 7, 1878.) Because he did not immediately espouse the cause of German-Americans in all their unreasonable quarrels and pretensions he was abused in newspapers and anarchistic addresses. One German-American, who had been living for several years at Lübeck, demanded to be exempted from the sanitary law requiring the vaccination of his child, another requested the legation to divorce him from his wife, and still another who had acquired American citizenship in order to avoid military duty, and who never intended to return to the United States, forwarded a gross attack upon the legation, which he had himself written, the day before he called for assistance.

The Princess Marie of Weimar once said to Bayard Taylor : " I have just read De Tocqueville's ' Democracy in America ; ' is it a correct account of your institutions ? "   Being assured that it was, she said, " But I am told by Americans that it is quite false, that everything has in reality changed and degenerated."   " Were they native-born Americans or German-Americans that told you this ? " asked Taylor, and learned in reply, as he suspected, that they belonged to the latter class.   " This class of German - Americans," Taylor frequently said, " has done us positive harm in Europe, where their expressions are welcome in reactionary circles."

Mr. H. Sidney Everett, the first secretary of the German legation, has very kindly written for me his recollections of Bayard Taylor as minister, and his report leaves nothing to be desired as a revelation of the admirable traits of character that showed bravely in the last desperate struggle for life.

" When the news of the appointment of Mr.
Taylor as Minister to Berlin reached me through
the newspapers, which is the courteous way the
Department of State adopts to inform its diplomatic and consular officers of any change, I had
been in charge of the legation there for some
months, and in a constant state of anxiety as to
what kind of a chief I was destined to have.
Several names of possible plenipotentiaries, each
less reassuring than the last, had reached me,
and the question had assumed an importance
which no one who has not, like myself, had five
different ministers to work under can appreciate.
But when the time of meeting at the train arrived, and my fate stood before me, all doubts
and fears vanished, and I knew by a glance at
that genial face, and after that cordial greeting,
that Mr. Taylor and I would pull together and
be warm friends, nor had I any occasion for a
moment to modify that impression.

" I had previously known Mr. Taylor only as
the author of ' Views Afoot,' which had stag-
gered me with its secrets of traveling on twenty-
five cents a day to more purpose than I had
been able to do on the same sum per hour.
Per contra, I may state that this same ' Views
Afoot ' was the innocent cause of my spending
various sums on indigent would-be travelers,
whose imagination had been fired by reading

those charming pages, and who, in endeavoring to repeat the experiment, had forgotten that they had not Mr. Taylor's brains.

" When Mr. Taylor reached Berlin, the warm weather was approaching and the diplomats were scattering to mountain and seaside resorts. My own family left for the Isle of Wight, and, as the legation offices, after the foreign custom, were then in my own residence, I moved into bachelor quarters, and gave up my apartment to Mr. Taylor and his family. Soon afterwards the ladies of his family went to the Thuringian Forest for the summer, where Mr. Taylor followed them when the legation duties permitted. Mr. Taylor's health, from the moment of his arrival, seemed to me far from what it ought to be for a man of his large and robust build ; but I hoped that the benefit of a sea voyage, with the change of climate and food in a country so familiar and congenial to him as Germany, would soon be apparent, especially as his physician apparently treated his troubles lightly and encouragingly. But such was not to be the case, and it was painful to watch the steady change in his condition for the worse, culminating in his decease within the year. How far he himself realized his condition, I was never able to ascertain, as he, to the last, replied to all inquiries that he should soon be quite well, and appeared to rely confidently on his splendid constitution and family longevity.

" In his official relations with his subordinates Mr. Taylor was as charming as in his private intercourse. While excelling in his own share of the work, and astonishing one with the ability and correctness with which he would grasp the true aspect of a question, and the fluency with which he would put it into good, clear English in his own model handwriting, without a rough draft, pause, alteration, or erasure, he never omitted an opportunity of allowing his secretaries to do themselves credit, and to assist him. He was never unreasonable or exacting. His thorough knowledge of the language, literature, and history of Germany enabled him to meet its rulers and people in a spirit that, while it conciliated them, obtained for our government better results than the aggressive spread-eagleism so often mistaken for diplomacy by our representatives. It was no wonder that every German heart was prepared to welcome the best translator of Goethe's ' Faust,' and the diplomatic corps cordially responded to a colleague who could address each of them in his own language, even to the representative of the Celestial Empire, who was then the latest addition to the diplomatic circle.

" Mr. Taylor's constant cheerfulness and deep sense of humor lightened the most arduous work, and after office hours a delightful drive by his side in his comfortable landau, listening to a steady flow of anecdote, poetical recitation, and traveler's experiences, was a perfect rest and treat for any one. It had been the rule in the legation, handed down from the incumbency of Mr. Davis, the bitterest foe to tobacco in all its forms, that there should be no smoking in the legation during office hours. In this Mr. Taylor, though an inveterate smoker, cheerfully acquiesced and never transgressed it, but as the hands of the clock pointed to the hour of closing, he would sit with a cigar in one hand and a match in the other, and at the first stroke would say, ' Now may I light it ? ' On the morning after his departure to the mountains I found a box of cigars on the office table ' with Mr. Taylor's kind regards,' and a line to say that his carriage was at my service. Such attentions are seldom experienced and never forgotten.

" Mr. Taylor's trip to the mountains was greatly shortened, and its benefits neutralized, by the advent of General Grant, and the meeting of the Berlin Congress, which necessitated his presence in the city at the hottest period of the year, and much fatigue and late hours. This was followed by the annoyance of furnishing and moving into his new residence and legation, which was the same one occupied both by his predecessor, Mr.

Davis, and his successor, Mr. White. The family were in the new quarters by November, and it was soon apparent that the hope of Mr. Taylor's recovery was a very faint one, and that all the best medical skill of Berlin could do for him was in vain. But to the last he was patient and cheerful, kept an eye on the official work, received his friends, wrote and read a little, painted a little, and finally dropped off quietly to his last sleep while sitting in his armchair in his library. One of his last pleasures was receiving the presentation copies of his new poem, ' Deukalion,' from his New York publishers. His last words to me were to ask if there was any official business requiring his attention, and before night he passed away with his devoted wife and daughter by his side.

" Could any consolation for his family have been possible, it would have been from the numerous and sincere expressions of respect and sympathy from the imperial family, officials, and friends, and from the press of both countries, which immediately poured in. Of the touching funeral ceremonies in the darkened banquet hall and the mournful procession to the tomb I have only a confused recollection, but when I turned from the cemetery on my homeward way I felt that I had lost a true friend, and that I could never have such another chief."

The round of dinners and the excitement attendant upon Taylor's departure from America had told disastrously upon him. He suffered intense pain, which his physicians were unable or unwilling to explain. At first they located the seat of the trouble in the colon, which led Taylor to groan, " Oh, that this trouble with the colon would come to — a period."

His intention to visit Carlsbad was defeated by the pressing business of the Berlin Congress, and by the presence of General Grant, to whom he was obliged to show social attentions. Work and worry had broken down the full power of his physical structure. That his vital forces were overburdened was first shown in the stooping shoulders and the drawn face, and later became terribly evident. He was, by nature, at all points splendidly endowed ; he had magnificent appetite and digestion, he could eat and drink freely and go at once to his desk and to work. Sickness was a positive humiliation to him as it was to Goethe.

There is a cruel and inscrutable irony at times in human destiny. Taylor at last had reached the solid ground upon which he could build his fame. His work lay easily before him, when in an instant it was snatched from his hand. It is the cry of Paracelsus again : —

" Ah, the curse, Aprile, Aprile !
    We get so near — so very, very near !
    'T is an old tale : Jove strikes the Titans down,
    Not when they set about their mountain-piling,
    But when another rock would crown the work."

Hegel is nearing the completion of his great
work when he is stricken with cholera. Fichte
kisses his dying wife, and the poison communi-
cates itself to him, and the great philosophy is
left unfinished.

Taylor possessed a kind of fatalism in regard
to his destiny, and his belief that man was immortal until his work was done no doubt sustained him with hope in his last hours. Professor Waterman T. Hewett has told me that
during Bayard Taylor's last visit to Ithaca, in
the spring and early summer of 1877, he spoke
with freedom and clearness concerning his
plans. " He told me," says Professor Hewett,
" that it was then his purpose to lecture for two
years more, the proceeds of which would enable
him to devote himself uninterruptedly to work
upon his ' Life of Goethe.' He estimated that
it would take about two years to write it after
the preliminary studies had been made and the
composition actually begun. I said to him that
if this were my work I could not rest until it
was accomplished ; it would be impossible for
me to contemplate the work from a distance,
without entering upon it. ' I should fear that

it would never be completed, that it would drop from my hands before it was finished.' 'On the contrary,' said Mr. Taylor, 'to have something before one to look forward to is the best guarantee of life. When I was a young man there was a certain work which I wished to achieve before I was thirty, and I could see nothing in my life beyond that date. I believed that my life would come to an end at that time. But as the time approached I gradually conceived the plan of translating "Faust." This I thought would occupy me until I was forty and I could see nothing before me after that time. But during the progress of this work I formed the purpose of writing the Life of Goethe, and now I believe that my life will be spared until it is accomplished. To have something before one to accomplish is the best assurance of life.'"

His great pain he bore patiently and without complaint. On the 17th of December the final change came. On the 19th his mind wandered and he was restless. He slept fitfully. At one instant he looked up with a look of surprise, and in a semi-whisper said, "I must be away." They were the last words of the Pilgrim of Eternity. Directly after he fell asleep, and at four o'clock in the afternoon he died, seated in the armchair in his library, which was also the office of the legation.

The funeral ceremonies were conducted by the Rev. J. P. Thompson. Berthold Auerbach spoke as though to the released spirit of his friend and fellow writer: "Thou wast born in the fatherland of Benjamin Franklin; and, like him, thou didst work thy way upward from a condition of lowly labor to be an apostle of the spirit of purity and freedom, and a representative of thy people among a foreign people. No, not among a foreign people: thou art as one of ourselves; thou hast died in the country of Goethe, to whose lofty spirit thou didst ever turn with devotion; thou hast erected a monument to him before thy people, and wouldst erect before all peoples another, which, alas! is lost with thee. But thou thyself wast and art one of those whom he foretold, a disciple of a universal literature, in which, high above all bounds of nationality, in the free, limitless ether, the purely human soars on daring pinions sunwards in ever new poetic forms. . . . Born in the New World, ripened in the Old, — and alas! severed so early from the tree of life! — thou didst teach thy people the history of the German people, that they, being brothers, should know one another; we bear that in our memories. Thou didst put into words of song thy people's outburst of joy at their centennial festival; when it returns again, and our own mortal frames lie motionless like thine here before us, then from millions of lips yet unborn will resound again the name of BAYARD TAYLOR. Thy memory shall be blessed!"

The remains were brought to America, March 13, 1879. At the New York City Hall, where the body lay in state, a dirge was sung by the German societies, and an oration was delivered by the Hon. Algernon S. Sullivan. Escorted by a guard of honor from the Koltes Post, Grand Army of the Republic, the remains were taken to the railway station and removed to Cedarcroft. There addresses were made by the Rev. Wm. H. Furness and Dr. Franklyn Taylor. The German and American flags were draped at the Unicorn in Kennett.

The funeral procession proceeded for three miles through the beautiful land that he had celebrated in the "Pennsylvania Pastorals" to the Quaker burial ground at Longwood.

> "Here Lowell came, in radiant youth,
>   A soul of fixed endeavor,
> Here Parker spake with lips of truth
>   That soon were closed forever."

At the grave the Rev. Dr. H. N. Powers read the funeral service, and a few words were said by the Rev. Dr. Furness and Mr. E. C. Stedman. A burial ode was sung by a Kennett chorus.

His grave is marked by a Greek altar, bearing the words, " He being dead yet speaketh." The bronze medallion on the tomb, surmounted by a wreath of oak leaves and bay, is by Launt Thompson. Upon the reverse of the circular stone are the lines from " Prince Deukalion:" —

> " For life whose source not here began
> Must fill the utmost sphere of man,
> And, so expanding, lifted be
> Along the line of God's decree,
> To find in endless growth all good, —
> In endless toil, beatitude."

All the poets he had loved paid tributes of affection to his memory. Longfellow, referring to the scene in the library of Taylor's Berlin home, wrote : —

> " Dead he lay among his books !
> The peace of God was in his looks.
>
> " As the statues in the gloom
> Watch o'er Maximilian's tomb,
>
> " So those volumes from their shelves
> Watched him, silent as themselves.
>
> " Ah ! his hand will nevermore
> Turn their storied pages o'er ;
>
> " Nevermore his lips repeat
> Songs of theirs, however sweet.
>
> " Let the lifeless body rest !
> He is gone, who was its guest ;

" Gone, as travelers haste to leave
　　An inn, nor tarry until eve.

" Traveler ! in what realms afar,
　　In what planet, in what star,

" In what vast, aerial space,
　　Shines the light upon thy face ?

" In what gardens of delight
　　Rest thy weary feet to-night ?

" Poet ! thou, whose latest verse
　　Was a garland on thy hearse ;

" Thou hast sung, with organ tone,
　　In Deukalion's life, thine own ;

" On the ruins of the Past
　　Blooms the perfect flower at last.

" Friend ! but yesterday the bells
　　Rang for thee their loud farewells ;

" And to-day they toll for thee,
　　Lying dead beyond the sea ;

" Lying dead among thy books,
　　The peace of God in all thy looks ! "

E. C. Stedman, R. H. Stoddard, George H. Calvert, and George H. Boker wrote their " In Memoriam " verses for a knightly comrade who was without fear and without reproach. Christopher P. Cranch, in his sonnet, recognizes Bayard Taylor's purity of character and loftiness of ambition : —

"Can one so strong in hope, so rich in bloom
That promised fruit of nobler worth than all
He yet had given, drop thus with sudden fall?
The busy brain no more its work resume?
Can death for life so versatile find room?
Still must we fancy thou canst hear our call
Across the sea — with no dividing wall
More dense than space to interpose its doom.
Ah then — farewell, young-hearted genial friend!
Farewell, true poet, who didst grow and build
From thought to thought still upward and still new.
Farewell, unsullied toiler in a guild
Where some defile their hands and where so few
With aims as pure strive faithful to the end."

I have reserved to the last Thomas Bailey Aldrich's exquisite monody, whose faultless lines speak for us the benediction and the praise with which we take leave of one of the bravest and gentlest of those who by desert in service have won high and secure places in the history of literature.

BAYARD TAYLOR.

In other years — lost youth's enchanted years,
Seen now, and evermore, through blinding tears
And empty longing for what may not be —
The Desert gave him back to us; the Sea
Yielded him up; the icy Norland strand
Lured him not long, nor that soft German air
He loved could keep him. Ever his own land
Fettered his heart and brought him back again.
What sounds are these of farewell and despair
Borne on the winds across the wintry main!

What unknown way is this that he is gone,
Our Bayard, in such silence and alone?
What new strange quest has tempted him once more
To leave us?   Vainly, standing by the shore,
We strain our eyes.   But patience! when the soft
Spring gales are blowing over Cedarcroft,
Whitening the hawthorn; when the violets bloom
Along the Brandywine, and overhead
The sky is blue as Italy's, he will come . . .
In the wind's whisper, in the swaying pine,
In song of bird and blossoming of vine,
And all fair things he loved ere he was dead!

APPENDIX.

BIBLIOGRAPHY OF BAYARD TAYLOR.

I. WORKS.

Ximena, or the Battle of the Sierra Morena, and other Poems. Philadelphia, Herman Hooker. 1844. 12mo.
  [This volume was suppressed afterwards by its author.]

Views Afoot; or Europe seen with Knapsack and Staff. With a preface by N. P. Willis. In two parts. New York, Wiley & Putnam. 1846. 12mo.

Rhymes of Travel, Ballads and Poems. New York, Geo. P. Putnam. 1849.
  [Really published in December, 1848.]

Eldorado, or, Adventures in the Path of Empire. With illustrations by the author. In two volumes. New York, Geo. P. Putnam. [May] 1850. London, Richard Bentley. 1850. 12mo.

A Book of Romances, Lyrics and Songs. Boston, Ticknor, Reed and Fields. 1851. 16mo.

A Journey to Central Africa, or Life and Landscapes from Egypt to the Negro Kingdoms of the White Nile. With a map and illustrations by the author. New York, G. P. Putnam & Co. [August] 1854. 12mo.

The Lands of the Saracen; or Pictures of Palestine, Asia Minor, Sicily and Spain. New York, G. P. Putnam & Co.; London, Sampson Low, Son & Co. [October] 1854. 12mo.

Poems of the Orient. Boston, Ticknor and Fields. [October 27] 1854. 16mo.

A Visit to India, China, and Japan in the Year 1853. New York, G. P. Putnam & Co.; London, Sampson Low, Son & Co. [September] 1855. 12mo.

Poems of Home and Travel. Boston, Ticknor and Fields. [November] 1855. 16mo.

Views Afoot. Revised edition with a new preface. New York. [November] 1855. 12mo.

Cyclopædia of Modern Travel. Cincinnati, Moore, Willstach, Keys & Co. 1856. 8vo.

Northern Travel: Summer and Winter Pictures of Sweden, Denmark, and Lapland. New York, G. P. Putnam; London, Sampson Low, Son & Co. 1857. 12mo.

Travels in Greece and Russia, with an Excursion to Crete. New York, G. P. Putnam; London, Sampson Low, Son & Co. 1859. 12mo.

At Home and Abroad: A Sketch-Book of Life, Scenery and Men. New York, G. P. Putnam; London, Sampson Low, Son & Co. [November] 1859. 12mo.

Cyclopædia of Modern Travel. Cincinnati. 1860. Revised and enlarged edition, 2 vols.

At Home and Abroad, II. Series. New York, G. P. Putnam. 1862. 12mo.

The Poet's Journal. Boston, Ticknor and Fields; London, Sampson Low & Co. [December] 1862. 12mo.

Hannah Thurston, A Story of American Life. New York, G. P. Putnam; London, Sampson Low & Co. [November] 1863. 12mo.

The Poems of Bayard Taylor. [Blue and Gold edition.] Boston, Ticknor and Fields. [October] 1864. 12mo.

John Godfrey's Fortunes: Related by Himself. A Story of American Life. New York, G. P. Putnam; London, Sampson Low, Son & Co. [November] 1864. 12mo.

Poems. Cabinet edition. 1865.

The Story of Kennett. New York, G. P. Putnam; London, Sampson Low, Son & Co. [March] 1866. 12mo.

The Picture of St. John. Boston, Fields, Osgood & Co. [October] 1866. 12mo.

Colorado: A Summer Trip. New York, G. P. Putnam & Son. [January] 1867. 12mo.

The Golden Wedding. A Masque. Privately printed. Philadelphia, J. B. Lippincott & Co. 1868. 16mo.

By-Ways of Europe. New York, G. P. Putnam & Son. 1869.

Views Afoot. New edition. Revised by the author, for Low's copyright cheap editions of American Books. London, Sampson Low, Son, and Marston. 1869. 12mo.

Joseph and His Friend. New York, G. P. Putnam. [November 24] 1870. 12mo.

Faust, A Tragedy, by Johann Wolfgang von Goethe. Part I. Translated in the Original Metres, by Bayard Taylor. Boston, Fields, Osgood & Co. [December] 1870.

Translation of Faust, Part II. Boston, James R. Osgood & Co. [March 25] 1871. Q.

Faust, Parts I. and II. London, Strahan & Co. [July] 1871. 8vo.

Faust, Part I. Leipzig, F. A. Brockhaus. [November or December] 1871. 8vo.

The Masque of the Gods. Boston, James R. Osgood & Co. [April 10] 1872. 12mo.

Beauty and the Beast, and Tales of Home. New York, G. P. Putnam & Sons. [April 9] 1872. 12mo.

Lars: a Pastoral of Norway. Boston, James R. Osgood & Co. [March 1, 1873. London, Strahan & Co. (March 8) 1873]. 12mo.

The Prophet. A Tragedy. Boston, James R. Osgood & Co. [September 13] 1874. 12mo.

Egypt and Iceland in the Year 1874. New York, G. P. Putnam's Sons. [October] 1874. 12mo.

A School History of Germany: from the Earliest Period to the Establishment of the German Empire in 1871. With one hundred and twelve illustrations and six historical maps. New York, D. Appleton & Co. 1874. 8vo.

Home Pastorals, Ballads and Lyrics. Boston, James R. Osgood & Co. [October] 1875. 12mo.

Faust. Kennett edition. Boston, J. R. Osgood & Co. 1875.

The Echo Club and other Literary Diversions. Boston, J. R. Osgood & Co. [July] 1876. 16mo.

Boys of Other Countries; Stories for American Boys. New York, G. P. Putnam's Sons. 1876. 8vo.

The National Ode, in facsimile.　Boston, J. R. Osgood & Co.
　　1876. ʹ 8vo.

Faust, Part II.　Leipzig, F. A. Brockhaus.　1876.　8vo.

Prince Deukalion, A Lyrical Drama.　Boston, Houghton, Os-
　　good & Co.; London, Trübner & Co. [November] 1878.　8vo.

Studies in German Literature, with an Introduction by George
　　H. Boker.　New York.　1879.　12mo.

Critical Essays, and Literary Notes.　New York, G. P. Put-
　　nam's Sons.　1880.　12mo.

The Poetical Works of Bayard Taylor.　Household Edition.
　　Boston, Houghton, Osgood and Co.　1880.　12mo.

The Dramatic Works of Bayard Taylor, with notes by Marie
　　Hansen-Taylor.　Boston, Houghton, Mifflin & Co.　1880.
　　12mo.

A History of Germany from the earliest times to the present
　　day, with an additional chapter by Marie Hansen-Taylor.
　　New York, D. Appleton & Co.　1894.　8vo.

II. CHRONOLOGY OF THE "POEMS OF THE ORIENT."

*(From the dates given by Bayard Taylor in the manuscript book
in the possession of Mr. Richard Henry Stoddard.)*

Smyrna.　October, 1851.

To a Persian Boy.　October, 1851.　(Written at Smyrna.)

The Nilotic Drinking Song.　January 9, 1852.　(Written on
　　the Nile, in Ethiopia.)

Kilimandjaro.　January, 1852.　(White Nile.)

The Orient.　July, 1852.　(Constantinople.)

Mimosa Blooms.　November, 1852.　(Cadiz.)

The Garden of Irem.　November, 1852.　(Granada.)

The Poet in the East.　February, 1853.

Aurum Potabile.　February, 1853.

The Arab Warrior.　March, 1853.

On the Sea.　March, 1853.

Arab to the Palm.　July, 1853.

The Goblet.　August, 1853.

Khalil.   August, 1853.

Arab Prayer.   September, 1853.

Requiem in the South.   September, 1853.

Nubia.   September, 1853.

Birth of the Horse.   September, 1853.

Charmian.   September, 1853.

Hymn to Air.   October, 1853.

Angel of Patevin.   October 15, 1853.

Desert Hymn to the Sun.   October 16, 1853.

Voyage of a Dream.   October 22, 1853.

Saturday Night at Sea.   October 23, 1853.

Gulistan.   October 24, 1853.

Ural Winter.   October 24, 1853.

Bedouin Song.   October 29, 1853.

Shekh.   October 30, 1853.

Amran's Wooing.   November 4, 1853.   (Written off the Cape of Good Hope.)

Birth of the Prophet.   November 29, 1853.

Morning at Tyre.   December 7, 1853.

A Picture.   December 15, 1853.

Jerusalem.   December 16, 1853.

Lament.   October 12, 1854.

III. CHRONOLOGICAL LIST OF WRITINGS.

A Visit to the Battle-ground of Brandywine.   (Published in the "Register," West Chester.)   1840.

Soliloquy of a Young Poet.   Published in "Saturday Evening Post," Philadelphia.   (Nine poems written, three published.)   1841.

Eleven poems written, two of them published in his first volume.   Rosalie (Ximena) in progress.   The Artist of Ravenna, and other prose written for a Bucks County paper.   1842.

About seventeen poems written and Rosalie completed.   1843.

Twenty-six poems, some translated from the German.   Letters of Travel to Philadelphia, "Saturday Evening Post," and "United States Gazette."   1844.

Ximena. 1844.

Thirty-two poems; some translations; letters of travel. 1845.

Letters for " Saturday Evening Post " and " Tribune." About twenty poems. Views Afoot. 1846.

Eight poems. The Demon of the Mirror, and editorials and reviews for the " Phœnixville Pioneer." 1847.

Twenty-four poems : among them the first California Ballads, published anonymously in the " Literary World," The Ode to Shelley and The Continents. Letters from New York to " Pioneer " and " Saturday Evening Post." Reviews for " Graham's Magazine." A tale, La Fioraja. (" Union Magazine.") Sketches for " The Opal." Rhymes of Travel. 1848.

Ten poems. Ariel, Kubleh, Odalisque, Storm Lines, Taurus, I plucked for Thee, Pine Forest of Monterey. Letters of Travel for " Tribune." Translation of " Raphael." 1849.

Twenty poems, among them Manuela, Hylas, From the Bosom of Ocean. Lecture, " The Animal Man." Eldorado. 1850.

Eleven poems. Letters of Travel in " Tribune." Cyclopædia of Literature and Art. Book of Romances. 1851.

Nine poems. Letters of Travel to " Tribune." 1852.

Thirty-three poems. " Tribune " letters. 1853.

Fourteen poems. Three lectures. Journey to Central Africa. Lands of the Saracen. Poems of the Orient. 1854.

Twelve poems. " Tribune " letters. Visit to India, China, and Japan. Poems of Home and Travel. 1855.

Four poems. " Tribune " letters. Cyclopædia of Travel. 1856.

" Tribune " letters. Northern Travel. 1857.

Three poems. " Tribune " letters. Lecture on " Moscow." 1858.

Nine poems. Short papers for New York " Mercury." Introduction to Stoddard's Life of Humboldt. Travels in Greece and Russia. At Home and Abroad. 1859.

Thirty-five poems (?). Papers about California in New York " Mercury." Confessions of a Medium. (" Atlantic

Monthly," vol. 6: 699.) Papers for "Independent." An Interview with Martin Luther, in "Harper's Magazine," January, 1861. 1860.

Seven poems. The Haunted Shanty. ("Atlantic Monthly," vol. 8: 57.) The Experiences of the A. C. ("Atlantic Monthly," vol. 9: 170.) The German Burns. A German Shooting Match. A Walk through the Franconian Switzerland. A Home in the Thuringian Forest. The Chiropodist. ("Harper's Magazine," March, 1862.) One of My Predecessors. Ernst II. of Saxe Coburg-Gotha. (Published in "Harper's Magazine," November, 1861.) 1861.

Friend Eli's Daughter. ("Atlantic Monthly," vol. 10: 99; "Eng. Dom. Monthly," vol. 21: 17, 74. "Sharpe," vol. 37: 244.)

A Cruise on Lake Ladoga. At Home and Abroad, II. Series. The Poet's Journal. 1862.

A Poem: The Neva. Hannah Thurston. Lecture: Russia and her People. 1863.

Six poems. John Godfrey's Fortunes. Thackeray. ("Atlantic," vol. 13: 371.) Between Europe and Asia. Lecture, Ourselves and our Relations. Poems. "Blue and Gold" edition. 1864.

Eleven poems. (Seven sonnets.) Winter Life in St. Petersburg. The Author of "Saul." Beauty and the Beast (written). 1865.

Four poems. The Little Post Boy. The Pasha's Son. The Two Herd Boys. Friedrich Rückert. ("Atlantic," vol. 18: 33.) A Distinguished Character. Letters to the "Tribune" from Colorado. Lecture, "American Life." Introduction to Frithjof's Saga. The Strange Friend. ("Atlantic," vol. 19: 54.) Review of Swinburne. ("North American Review," 104: 287.) The Story of Kennett. The Picture of St. John. 1866.

Two poems. Travel in the United States. The Little Land of Appenzell. ("Atlantic," 20: 213.) From Perpignan to Montserrat. A Visit to the Balearic Islands. ("Atlantic," 20: 680; 21: 73.) Catalonian Bridle Roads. The Repub-

lic of the Pyrenees. The Grande Chartreuse. The Kyffhäuser and its Legends. Twenty letters to the "Tribune."
Colorado : A Summer Trip. 1867.

Nine poems, including the German dedication, An Goethe.
Faust, Part I., completed. Letters for the "Tribune." A
Week on Capri. ("Atlantic," vol. 21 : 740.) A Trip to
Ischia. ("Atlantic," vol. 22 : 155.) The Island of Mad-
dalena. ("Atlantic," vol. 22 : 326.) The Land of Paoli.
("Atlantic," vol. 22 : 611.) The Teutoburger Forest. The
Swabian Alb. Mural Paintings of Pompeii. ("Putnam,"
vol. 12 : 1.) Can a Life Hide Itself ? ("Atlantic," vol. 23 :
605.) Mrs. Strongitharm's Report. ("Galaxy," vol. 8 :
811.) Contributions to "Hearth and Home." The Golden
Wedding, a Masque. 1868.

Eleven poems, including the Gettysburg Ode, and the August
Pastoral, "Literature, Art, and Science" for "Putnam's
Magazine." Preface, To the English Reader, in Views
Afoot. Introduction to the English translation of Auer-
bach's "Villa on the Rhine." Jacob Flint's Journey. Lec-
ture on "Reform and Art." Address at the Dedication of
the Halleck Monument. Reviews for the "Tribune." By-
Ways of Europe. 1869.

Five poems, among them the German "Jubellied." The
"Rhine-Guard," translated. Notes for "Faust." "Lit-
erature, Art, and Science," for "Putnam's." Joseph and
His Friend. Lectures on German Literature. Reviews for
"Tribune." Letters for "Tribune." "Faust," Part I.,
published. 1870.

Five poems. Twin-Love. ("Atlantic," vol. 28 : 257.) Paper
on Humboldt. ("Harper's Weekly.") Lectures on German Literature. Down the Eastern Shore. ("Harper's
Weekly.") The Northwest Letters. ("Tribune.") Sights
in and around Yedo. ("Scribner's," vol. 13 : 132.) The
Heart of Arabia. ("Scribner's," vol. 3 : 545.) Editorial
work on Library of Travel, for "Scribner's." "Faust,"
Part II., published. Introduction and Dialogues of the
Echo Club. 1871.

Eighteen poems. Amerikanische Dichter und Dichtkunst. The Masque of the Gods. Beauty and the Beast. Lars (written). 1872.

Eight poems. Twelve letters for the "Tribune." Two articles for "Tribune." An article in "Neue Freie Presse" of Vienna. School History of Germany (written). Who was She? ("Atlantic," vol. 34 : 257.) Lars (published). 1873.

Six poems. Ancient Troy (in "Tribune"). Egypt Revisited. (Eleven letters in "Tribune.") African Exploration. (Two articles for "Tribune.") The Fayoom. Letters from Iceland (for "Tribune"). Ancient Egypt. (A Lecture.) The Prophet, A Tragedy. Egypt and Iceland. School History of Germany (published). 1874.

About six poems, and Prince Deukalion begun. Lecture on Jean Paul Richter. Letters about the Bunker Hill Celebration for "Tribune." Alongshore. (Six letters for the "Tribune.") Lecture, Literature as an Art. Ion of Iceland. ("St. Nicholas.") Reviews of Books for the "International Review," and "Tribune." Article on Schiller for Johnson's Cyclopædia. Edits "Picturesque Europe" (D. Appleton). Home Pastorals. 1875.

Ten poems. The Young Serf. ("St. Nicholas Magazine.") June Days at Weimar. ("Atlantic," vol. 39 : 61.) An Impossible Story. ("Scribner's," vol. 16 : 131.) Letters for "Cincinnati Commercial." The Echo Club. Boys of Other Countries. 1876.

Five poems. Translation of Schiller's "Don Carlos." Alfred Tennyson. ("International Review," vol. 4 : 397.) Historical Introduction to "Bismarck" by Geo. Hezekiel. Letters for "Cincinnati Commercial." The Halleck Statue. ("North American Review," vol. 125 : 60.) Ephesus, Cyprus, Mycenæ. ("North American Review," vol. 126 : 111.) Letters from White Sulphur Springs. ("Tribune.") Susan Lane's Christmas. ("Weekly Tribune.") Studies of Animal Nature. ("Atlantic Monthly," vol. 39 : 135.) 1877.

Four poems. Contributions to "Tribune." Life and Habits Abroad. ("Semi-Weekly Tribune.") Prince Deukalion. 1878.

INDEX.